LEARN CHINESE
VOCABULARY
FOR INTERMEDIATE

NEW HSK LEVEL 5 VOCABULARY BOOK
MASTER 1000+ WORDS IN CONTEXT

Chinese • Pinyin • English

LingLing

www.linglingmandarin.com

My gratitude goes to my wonderful students who study Mandarin with me. You have inspired my writing and provided me with valuable feedback to complete this book. Your support is deeply appreciated!

A special thanks goes to my husband, Phil, who motivated my creation and assisted with editing the book.

Access
FREE AUDIO

SCAN ME

Check the **"ACCESS AUDIO"** chapter for
password and full instructions
(see Table of Contents)

CONTENTS

天 行 健
tiān　xíng　jiàn

君 子 以 自 强 不 息
jūn　zǐ　yǐ　zì　qiáng　bù　xī

As heaven's movement is ever vigorous,
so must a gentleman constantly strive for excellence.

- BOOK OF CHANGES -

INTRODUCTION

Great job on finishing the previous four levels of the **NEW HSK Vocabulary Series**! It takes great commitment to make it this far. Take some time to reflect on your accomplishments, that's over 3000 words in the bag! Keep up the great work. Now, get ready for Level 5, where you'll tackle over 1000 new Chinese words, a pivotal step forward in your intermediate language learning adventure.

The NEW HSK Intermediate Levels (4-6) will expand your Chinese vocabulary by over 3000 words, building upon the 2000 words from the Elementary Levels (1-3). Mastering levels 1-6 enables fluent and refined communication, opening doors to numerous opportunities in travel, work, deeper relationships, and personal growth.

WHAT IS THIS BOOK

This comprehensive vocabulary book for HSK 5 introduces more than 1000 essential modern Chinese words, setting the stage for confident and practical real-life conversations. As an intermediate learner, you will also explore more sophisticated words and phrases, especially beneficial in business or formal settings. Whether you're studying for HSK or not, rest assured that the core vocabulary and supplementary terms in this guide are carefully chosen for their practicality in modern Chinese communication, ensuring an effective and relevant learning experience.

All the keywords are presented in alphabetical order according to the pinyin, each featuring:

- Simplified Chinese characters used in Mainland China
- Pinyin for pronunciation aid
- English definitions
- Complete sentence examples demonstrating usage
- Full English translations
- Downloadable Chinese audio

BONUS CONTENT

Alongside helping you to master HSK Level 5 vocabulary, this book also includes a special chapter focused on enhancing grammar skills. This chapter covers 20 essential grammar points and widely used sentence structures, incorporating vocabulary from HSK Level 5. This integration ensures a seamless progression from learning individual words to constructing fluent, natural-sounding sentences, mirroring the way native speakers use the language.

HOW THIS BOOK WILL HELP

Mastering Chinese goes beyond simple word memorization. This book enhances vocabulary learning through practical examples, enabling you to grasp not only the words but also their contextual application, including typical sentence structures.

Engaging with these examples and rehearsing the sentence patterns will improve your proficiency in daily communication, travel, and business contexts. Regardless of your intention to take the HSK exam, this book will substantially improve your conversational skills.

LEVEL UP YOUR LEARNING WITH COMPANION BOOKS

I highly recommend complementing your learning with my book **Chinese Conversations for Intermediate**. It will immerse you in authentic everyday scenarios in modern China, enhancing your speaking and listening skills. It will serve as an indispensable companion for anyone aspiring to converse fluently in modern Chinese settings.

If you enjoy engaging stories and want to explore Chinese culture deeper through its legends, myths, and folktales then you should pick up **Chinese Stories for Language Learners: Intermediate**. It provides an entertaining approach to enrich your language skills while delving into the rich tapestry of Chinese cultural narratives.

FREE DOWNLOADABLE AUDIO

Great news! The Chinese audio files for the book is a FREE gift for you, which you can access from the Access Audio page (see table of contents). I strongly encourage you to download and use the audio as part of your learning with this book.

NEW HSK

HSK, short for Hanyu Shuiping Kaoshi (Mandarin Level Examination), is an internationally recognized skill test for non-native Chinese speakers. It is officially introduced by the Chinese government and organized by the Chinese Education Ministry Hanban/Confucius Institutes. The new HSK standard (HSK 3.0) was implemented in July 2021, replacing the old HSK Standard with its 6 levels. The new version features 9 levels, incorporating a more specific classification system, including levels and bands. Compared to its predecessor, the new HSK has been upgraded and expanded, with an increased number of words required for each level.

As a general learner, focusing on levels 1 to 6 will enable you to become an effective Mandarin speaker. Levels 7 and above are specifically designed for advanced learners, such as those intending to pursue Master's or PhD programs in Chinese language studies.

LEARN CHINESE WITH A NEW VISION

The Chinese language, which has evolved over 3500 years, embodies a rich diversity and artistic depth. As one of the most widely spoken languages globally, proficiency in Chinese unlocks a myriad of opportunities in travel, business, and personal development.

Learning Chinese, however, transcends mere language acquisition. It is an immersion into a distinctive cultural mindset and an avenue to broadening your worldview. Immersing yourself in its language and cultural nuances offers a deep appreciation of a heritage that has flourished for millennia.

HOW TO USE THIS BOOK

Here are some tips to use this book most effectively:

1. **Stick to a fixed routine**. For example, master ten words per day or week - you pick a number and schedule that suits you, but most importantly, stick to it.

2. **Capture the Words**. Write down the key vocabulary in a notebook or type it out digitally, this can enhance your memory of the characters.

3. **Read aloud**, especially the sentence examples. Imagine the context in your head when reading.

4. **Test** yourself by covering the Pinyin and English (using a bookmark for example). If you can read and understand the Chinese on its own, you have memorized it.

5. **Listen** to the audio. Practice imitating the audio and keep listening until you can comprehend the audio without the help of the text.

6. **Review** as often as you can. Repetition is the mother of skill!

7. **Create** your own sentence examples. Practice speaking them aloud, and if possible, use them with a language partner. One becomes a true master through creation!

BELIEVE IN YOURSELF

Never be afraid of making mistakes. In real life, even advanced learners and native speakers make mistakes! Learning from mistakes only makes us grow quicker! So, never let mistakes put you off. Instead, be bold, embrace and learn from them!

SET GOALS AND STAY COMMITTED

Have a committed learning attitude and set goals from small to big will lead you to great achievements in your Chinese learning journey. So stay committed and never give up! Just like this Chinese idiom:

yǒu	zhì	zhě	shì	jìng	chéng
有	志	者	事	竟	成

Nothing is impossible to a willing heart

1

VOCABULARY

IN CONTEXT

1 安慰 ān wèi
Verb: to comfort
Noun: comfort

Verb
tā gāng gāng shī yè le，wǒ děi ān wèi tā
他 刚 刚 失 业 了，我 得 **安 慰** 他 。
He just lost his job and I had **to comfort** him.

Noun
xiè xie nǐ de ān wèi，wǒ gǎn jué hǎo duō le
谢 谢 你 的 **安 慰**，我 感 觉 好 多 了 。
Thank you for your **comfort**, I feel much better.

2 岸 àn
Noun: river bank; shore

wǒ men de chuán kuài kào àn le
我 们 的 船 快 靠 **岸** 了 。
Our boat is almost near the **shore**.

3 岸上 àn shàng
Noun: ashore; on the shore

wǒ kàn dào tā yí gè rén zài àn shàng chōu yān
我 看 到 他 一 个 人 在 **岸 上** 抽 烟 。
I saw him smoking alone **on the shore**.

4 按摩 àn mó
Verb: to massage
Noun: massage

Verb
wǒ xǐ huān ràng lǎo zhāng àn mó wǒ de bèi
我 喜 欢 让 老 张 **按 摩** 我 的 背 。
I like to let Lao Zhang **massage** my back.

Noun
tā shì zhuān yè de àn mó shī
他 是 专 业 的 **按 摩** 师 。
He is a professional masseur (**massage** master).

5 拔 bá
Verb: to pluck; to pull out

wǒ ér zi qù tián lǐ bá luó bo le
我 儿 子 去 田 里 **拔** 萝 卜 了 。
My son went to the field **to pull (out)** radishes.

6　白酒　bái jiǔ

Noun: liquor; Chinese white wine

wǒ de kè hù sòng le wǒ yì píng míng pái bái jiǔ
我 的 客 户 送 了 我 一 瓶 名 牌 **白 酒** 。
My client gave me a bottle of brand-name **Chinese white wine**.

7　拜访　bài fǎng

Verb: to visit (formal)
Noun: visit

Verb
zǒng tǒng yào qù bài fǎng tuì yì lǎo bīng
总 统 要 去 **拜 访** 退 役 老 兵 。
The president is going **to visit** retired veterans.

Noun
tā men fēi cháng qī dài tā de bài fǎng
他 们 非 常 期 待 他 的 **拜 访** 。
They are looking forward to his **visit** very much.

8　版　bǎn

Noun: edition; version

zhè bù diàn yǐng de xīn bǎn xià gè yuè huì shàng yìng
这 部 电 影 的 新 **版** 下 个 月 会 上 映 。
The new **version** of the film will be released next month.

9　扮演　bàn yǎn

Verb: to play (role)

tā zài diàn yǐng lǐ bàn yǎn yí gè tiān shǐ
她 在 电 影 里 **扮 演** 一 个 天 使 。
She **plays** an angel in the movie.

10　棒　bàng

Noun: stick
Adjective: great; awesome

Noun
duì le nǐ huì dǎ bàng qiú ma
对 了 ， 你 会 打 **棒** 球 吗 ？
By the way, can you play baseball (**stick** ball)?

Adj.
wǒ de jiào liàn kě yǐ jiāo nǐ tā hěn bàng
我 的 教 练 可 以 教 你 ， 他 很 **棒** ！
My coach can teach you, he's **great**!

11　包围　bāo wéi　Verb: to surround

糟糕，他们被敌人包围了。
zāo gāo，tā men bèi dí rén bāo wéi le

Terrible, they're **surrounded** by enemies.

12　包装　bāo zhuāng　Verb: to pack; to wrap (commodities/goods)　Noun: package

Verb
那些工人负责包装产品。
nà xiē gōng rén fù zé bāo zhuāng chǎn pǐn

Those workers are responsible for **packing** the products.

Noun
其实，包装费比产品的成本高。
qí shí，bāo zhuāng fèi bǐ chǎn pǐn de chéng běn gāo

In fact, the **package** fee is higher than the product cost.

13　保卫　bǎo wèi　Verb: to defend

士兵们的任务是保卫国家。
shì bīng men de rèn wù shì bǎo wèi guó jiā

The mission of soldiers is **to defend** the country.

14　保养　bǎo yǎng　Verb: to maintain (tangible things)

用什么方法保养钻石戒指？
yòng shén me fāng fǎ bǎo yǎng zuàn shí jiè zhǐ

What method should I use **to maintain** a diamond ring?

15　报答　bào dá　Verb: to reciprocate; to repay (kindness)

他的养女觉得有必要报答他。
tā de yǎng nǚ jué de yǒu bì yào bào dá tā

His adopted daughter thinks it's necessary **to repay** him.

16 报警　bào jǐng　**Verb:** to call the police

tā yì tīng dào qiāng shēng jiù bào jǐng le
他 一 听 到 枪 声 就 **报 警** 了。
He **called the police** as soon as he heard the gunfire.

17 抱怨　bào yuàn　**Verb:** to complain
Noun: compliant

Verb

wǒ mā zǒng shì bào yuàn wǒ bà luō suo
我 妈 总 是 **抱 怨** 我 爸 啰 嗦。
My mum always **complains** that my dad's too talkative.

Noun

kě wǒ bà wán quán bú zài hu tā de bào yuàn
可 我 爸 完 全 不 在 乎 她 的 **抱 怨**。
But my dad doesn't care about her **complaints** at all.

18 背包　bēi bāo　**Noun:** backpack

zhè gè xīn bēi bāo huā le wǒ měi yuán
这 个 新 **背 包** 花 了 我 315 美 元。
This new **backpack** cost me $315.

19 悲剧　bēi jù　**Noun:** tragedy

wǒ xǐ huān kàn de shì xǐ jù bú shì bēi jù
我 喜 欢 看 的 是 喜 剧， 不 是 **悲 剧**。
What I like to watch is comedy, not **tragedy**.

20 悲伤　bēi shāng　**Adjective:** sorrowful
Noun: sadness; sorrow

Adj.

qī zi qù shì hòu tā fēi cháng bēi shāng
妻 子 去 世 后， 他 非 常 **悲 伤**。
After his wife passed away, he was very **sorrowful**.

Noun

wǒ néng tǐ huì tā de bēi shāng hé gū dú
我 能 体 会 他 的 **悲 伤** 和 孤 独。
I can relate to his **sadness** and loneliness.

21 北极   běi jí   **Noun:** arctic; the North Pole

dì qiú de nán jí hé běi jí yǒu duō yuǎn
地球的南极和**北极**有多远？
How far apart are the Earth's South Pole and **North Pole**?

22 被动   bèi dòng   **Adjective:** passive

zài gǎn qíng shàng tā yǒu diǎn bèi dòng bú gòu zhǔ dòng
在感情上他有点**被动**，不够主动。
In relationships, he is a bit **passive** and not proactive enough.

23 辈   bèi   **Noun:** generation

wǒ de fù mǔ bèi jié hūn de bǐ wǒ men zǎo
我的父母**辈**结婚得比我们早。
My parents' **generation** got married earlier than us.

24 本人   běn rén   **Noun:** oneself

wǒ běn rén jué de wǎn hūn bú shì huài shì
我**本人**觉得晚婚不是坏事。
I **myself** think that marrying later is not a bad thing.

25 鼻子   bí zi   **Noun:** nose

zhè tiáo gǒu de bí zi shì xīn xíng de
这条狗的**鼻子**是心形的！
This dog's **nose** is heart-shaped!

26 比方 bǐ fāng

Noun: example; analogy
Conjunction: suppose; for example

Noun
我 不 懂 ， 你 可 以 给 我 一 个 比 方 吗 ？
wǒ bù dǒng, nǐ kě yǐ gěi wǒ yí gè bǐ fāng ma
I don't understand, can you give me an **example**?

Conj.
他 小 气 ， 比 方 他 从 不 请 别 人 吃 饭 。
tā xiǎo qì, bǐ fāng tā cóng bù qǐng bié rén chī fàn
He is stingy, **for example**, he never treats others to meals.

27 比重 bǐ zhòng

Noun: proportion; specific gravity

制 造 业 在 这 里 的 经 济 比 重 很 大 。
zhì zào yè zài zhè lǐ de jīng jì bǐ zhòng hěn dà
The manufacturing sector constitutes a large **proportion** of the economy here.

28 彼此 bǐ cǐ

Pronoun: each other

我 们 是 十 年 的 好 友 ， 很 关 心 彼 此 。
wǒ men shì shí nián de hǎo yǒu, hěn guān xīn bǐ cǐ
We've been friends for 10 years and care about **each other**.

29 必 bì

Adverb: certainly; necessarily (formal)

如 果 我 需 要 帮 忙 ， 他 必 会 帮 我 。
rú guǒ wǒ xū yào bāng máng, tā bì huì bāng wǒ
If I need help, he will **certainly** help me.

30 必需   bì xū

Verb: to need (must)
Adjective: necessary

Verb
wǒ bì xū gěi tā yí gè hé lǐ de jiě shì
我 **必 需** 给 他 一 个 合 理 的 解 释。
I **must** give him a reasonable explanation.

Adj.
wèi le tí gāo xiào lǜ zhè xiàng cuò shī shì bì xū de
为 了 提 高 效 率, 这 项 措 施 是 **必 需** 的。
To increase efficiency, this measure is **necessary**.

31 毕竟   bì jìng

Adverb: after all

yào jiě jué bì jìng wèn tí cún zài hěn jiǔ le
要 解 决, **毕 竟** 问 题 存 在 很 久 了。
We must solve it, **after all** the issue has existed for a long time.

32 闭幕   bì mù

Verb: to close;
to finish (formal)

guó jì shāng wù lùn tán yǐ jīng bì mù le
国 际 商 务 论 坛 已 经 **闭 幕** 了。
The International Business Forum has **finished**.

33 闭幕式   bì mù shì

Noun: closing
ceremony

wǒ hěn róng xìng cān jiā le bì mù shì
我 很 荣 幸 参 加 了 **闭 幕 式**。
I was honored to attend the **closing ceremony**.

34 边境   biān jìng

Noun: border;
frontier

xī wàng zhèng fǔ néng hé píng jiě jué biān jìng wèn tí
希 望 政 府 能 和 平 解 决 **边 境** 问 题。
I hope the government can resolve the **border** issue peacefully.

35 编辑   biān jí   **Verb:** to edit
Noun: editor

Verb
gōng sī yǒu zhuān yuán biān jí wén běn hé shì pín
公 司 有 专 员 **编 辑** 文 本 和 视 频 。
The company has specialists who **edit** texts and videos.

Noun
chū bǎn shè yǒu hěn duō zhuān yè de biān jí
出 版 社 有 很 多 专 业 的 **编 辑** 。
The publisher has many professional **editors**.

36 变动   biàn dòng   **Noun:** change; variation

gǔ shì de biǎo xiàn hé jīng jì de biàn dòng yǒu guān
股 市 的 表 现 和 经 济 的 **变 动** 有 关 。
The performance of the stock market is related to **changes** in the economy.

37 便利   biàn lì   **Verb:** to facilitate
Noun: convenience

Verb
ān zhuāng wǎng luò shì wèi le biàn lì jū mín de shēng huó
安 装 网 络 是 为 了 **便 利** 居 民 的 生 活 。
Networks are installed **to facilitate** residents' lives.

Noun
zhè kě yǐ wèi tā men tí gōng wǎng gòu biàn lì
这 可 以 为 他 们 提 供 网 购 **便 利** 。
This provides them with the **convenience** of online shopping.

38 便条   biàn tiáo   **Noun:** sticky note

kāi huì de shí hòu wǒ yòng biàn tiáo jì lù xìn xī
开 会 的 时 候 ， 我 用 **便 条** 记 录 信 息 。
During meetings, I use **sticky notes** to record information.

39 便于   biàn yú   **Verb:** to make easy

zhè biàn yú zǒng jié huì yì de zhòng diǎn nèi róng
这 **便 于** 总 结 会 议 的 重 点 内 容 。
This **makes it easy** to summarize the key points of the meeting.

40 宾馆   bīn guǎn   **Noun:** hotel

^{zhè} ^{shì} ^{wǔ} ^{xīng} ^{jí} ^{bīn} ^{guǎn} ^{yì} ^{qiān} ^{měi} ^{yuán} ^{yì} ^{wǎn}
这 是 五 星 级 **宾 馆**, 一 千 美 元 一 晚。
This is a five-star **hotel**, costing $1000 a night.

41 饼   bǐng   **Noun:** pie; pastry

^{wǒ} ^{huì} ^{zuò} ^{píng} ^{guǒ} ^{bǐng} ^{tā} ^{huì} ^{zuò} ^{yīng} ^{táo} ^{bǐng}
我 会 做 苹 果 **饼**, 她 会 做 樱 桃 **饼**。
I can make apple **pie** and she can make cherry **pie**.

42 饼干   bǐng gān   **Noun:** biscuit; cookie

^{tā} ^{yǒu} ^{táng} ^{niào} ^{bìng} ^{bù} ^{néng} ^{chī} ^{tián} ^{bǐng} ^{gān}
他 有 糖 尿 病, 不 能 吃 甜 **饼 干**。
He has diabetes and cannot eat sweet **cookies**.

43 病毒   bìng dú   **Noun:** virus

^{fáng} ^{zhǐ} ^{bìng} ^{dú} ^{de} ^{màn} ^{yán} ^{shì} ^{shǒu} ^{yào} ^{rèn} ^{wù}
防 止 **病 毒** 的 蔓 延 是 首 要 任 务。
Preventing the spread of the **virus** is the top priority.

44 玻璃   bō li   **Noun:** glass

^{wǒ} ^{yào} ^{mǎi} ^{gāo} ^{zhì} ^{liàng} ^{de} ^{bō} ^{li} ^{chuāng}
我 要 买 高 质 量 的 **玻 璃** 窗。
I want to buy high quality **glass** windows.

45 博客   bó kè   **Noun:** blog

^{zhè} ^{gè} ^{bó} ^{zhǔ} ^{yǒu} ^{bǎi} ^{wàn} ^{fěn} ^{sī} ^{guān} ^{zhù} ^{tā} ^{de} ^{bó} ^{kè}
这 个 博 主 有 百 万 粉 丝 关 注 她 的 **博 客**。
This blogger has millions of fans following her **blog**.

46 博览会　　bó lǎn huì　　**Noun:** exhibition; exposition

wǒ zài bó lǎn huì shàng kàn dào le měi guó shǒu fù
我 在 **博 览 会** 上 看 到 了 美 国 首 富 。
I saw the richest man in America at the **exhibition**.

47 博士　　bó shì　　**Noun:** Ph.D.

tīng shuō　　tā shì jīng jì xué bó shì
听 说 ， 他 是 经 济 学 **博 士** 。
I heard that he has a **Ph.D.** in economics.

48 博物馆　　bó wù guǎn　　**Noun:** museum

nǐ qù guò lún dūn de dà yīng bó wù guǎn ma
你 去 过 伦 敦 的 大 英 **博 物 馆** 吗 ？
Have you been to the British **Museum** in London?

49 (薄)弱　　(bó) ruò　　**Adjective:** weak

tā dé ái zhèng le　　shēn tǐ yuè lái yuè bó ruò
他 得 癌 症 了 ， 身 体 越 来 越 **薄 弱** 。
He has cancer and his body's getting **weak**er and **weak**er.

tā céng jīng hěn ruò　　xiàn zài hěn qiáng
他 曾 经 很 **弱** ， 现 在 很 强 。
He was once **weak**, now he is strong.

50 不顾　　bú gù　　**Verb:** to disregard; to ignore

tā bú gù zì shēn ān quán qù jiù rén
他 **不 顾** 自 身 安 全 去 救 人 。
He **disregarded** his own safety to save others.

51 不利   bú lì   **Adjective:** unfavourable; disadvantageous

_{wǒ yào fēn bié kǎo lǜ yǒu lì hé bú lì de fāng miàn}
我要分别考虑有利和**不利**的方面。

I need to consider the advantageous and **disadvantegous** aspects separately.

52 不耐烦   bú nài fán   **Adjective:** impatient

_{jié hūn liǎng nián hòu tā duì lǎo pó bú nài fán le}
结婚两年后，他对老婆**不耐烦**了。

After 2 years of marriage, he became **impatient** with his wife.

53 不幸   bú xìng   **Adjective:** misfortune; unfortunate

_{péng yǒu men dōu quàn tā fàng qì zhè bú xìng de hūn yīn}
朋友们都劝她放弃这**不幸**的婚姻。

Friends all advised her to give up this **unfortunate** marriage.

54 不易   bú yì   **Adjective:** not easy; difficult; tough

_{shēng huó bú yì bǎo chí lè guān de xīn tài hěn zhòng yào}
生活**不易**，保持乐观的心态很重要。

Life is **not easy**, it's important to maintain an optimistic attitude.

55 补偿   bǔ cháng   **Verb:** to compensate   **Noun:** compensation

Verb
_{gōng sī yīng gāi bǔ cháng jiā bān de yuán gōng}
公司应该**补偿**加班的员工。

Companies should **compensate** employees for working overtime.

Noun
_{yě xǔ jiǎng jīn shì zuì hǎo de bǔ cháng fāng shì}
也许，奖金是最好的**补偿**方式。

Perhaps a bonus is the best means of **compensation**.

56 补贴　bǔ tiē　Noun: subsidy

rú guǒ zài jié jià rì jiā bān, yǒu bǔ tiē ma
如果在节假日加班，有补贴吗？
If working overtime on public holidays, is there any **subsidy**?

57 不曾　bù céng　Adverb: never (past events)

wǒ bù céng xiǎng guò huì zài hé qián nán yǒu yù dào
我不曾想过会再和前男友遇到。
I **never** thought I would meet my ex-boyfriend again.

58 不得了　bù dé liǎo　Phrase: how awful; no end of trouble

tā jū rán shuō hái ài wǒ, zhēn bù dé liǎo
他居然说还爱我，真不得了！
He actually said he still loves me, truly **no end of trouble**!

59 不敢当　bù gǎn dāng　Phrase: I don't deserve this (showing modesty)

bié shuō wǒ shì tiān cái, bù gǎn dāng
别说我是天才，不敢当！
Don't say I'm a genius, **I don't deserve this**!

60 不良　bù liáng　Adjective: bad; harmful; unhealthy

xī dú hé xù jiǔ dōu shì bù liáng xí guàn
吸毒和酗酒都是不良习惯。
Drug abuse and alcoholism are both **unhealthy** habits.

61 不免　bù miǎn　Adverb: inevitably; unavoidably

nǐ rú guǒ bù gǎi zhèng, tā bù miǎn huì shēng qì
你如果不改正，她不免会生气。
If you don't correct yourself, she'll **inevitably** be angry.

62 不能不

bù néng bù

Adverb: have to; cannot but

^{shì}事 ^{qíng}情 ^{tài}太 ^{yán}严 ^{zhòng}重， ^{wǒ}我 **^{bù}不 ^{néng}能 ^{bù}不** ^{hǎo}好 ^{hǎo}好 ^{sī}思 ^{kǎo}考。

The matter is too serious and I **have to** give it a good thought.

63 不时

bù shí

Adverb: from time to time

^{tā}他 ^{suī}虽 ^{rán}然 ^{yǒu}有 ^{nǚ}女 ^{péng}朋 ^{yǒu}友，^{què}却 **^{bù}不 ^{shí}时** ^{hé}和 ^{bié}别 ^{rén}人 ^{yuē}约 ^{pào}炮。

Although he has a girlfriend, he hooks up with others **from time to time.**

64 不停

bù tíng

Adverb: non-stop

^{zhēn}真 ^{shì}是 ^{zhā}渣 ^{nán}男，^{zǒng}总 ^{shì}是 **^{bù}不 ^{tíng}停** ^{de}地 ^{chū}出 ^{guǐ}轨！

What a scumbag, always cheating **non-stop**!

65 不许

bù xǔ

Verb: to forbid; to not allow

^{wǒ}我 ^{mā}妈 **^{bù}不 ^{xǔ}许** ^{wǒ}我 ^{bà}爸 ^{dǔ}赌 ^{bó}博 ^{hé}和 ^{chōu}抽 ^{yān}烟。

My mum **forbids** my dad from gambling or smoking.

66 不止

bù zhǐ

Verb: more than; not limited to

^{lǎo}老 ^{bǎn}板 ^{de}的 ^{tóu}投 ^{zī}资 **^{bù}不 ^{zhǐ}止** ^{fáng}房 ^{dì}地 ^{chǎn}产。

The boss' investments are **not limited to** real estate.

67 不足

bù zú

Adjective: insufficient

^{yóu}由 ^{yú}于 ^{zī}资 ^{jīn}金 **^{bù}不 ^{zú}足**， ^{yè}业 ^{wù}务 ^{wú}无 ^{fǎ}法 ^{yùn}运 ^{xíng}行。

Due to **insufficient** funds, the business is unable to operate.

68 部位   bù wèi   **Noun:** part (of body)

yī shēng zhèng zài jiǎn chá tā shòu shāng de bù wèi
医 生 正 在 检 查 他 受 伤 的 **部 位** 。
Doctors are examining his injured **part**.

69 猜   cāi   **Verb:** to guess

wǒ cāi tā shì qí mó tuō chē de shí hòu shòu shāng de
我 **猜** 他 是 骑 摩 托 车 的 时 候 受 伤 的 。
I **guess** he was injured while riding the motorbike.

70 猜测   cāi cè   **Verb:** to guess
                              Noun: guess; conjecture

Verb
wǒ cāi cè jīn róng wēi jī hěn kuài jiù huì guò qù
我 **猜 测** 金 融 危 机 很 快 就 会 过 去 。
I **guess** that the financial crisis will be over soon.

Noun
wǒ xī wàng nǐ de cāi cè shì zhèng què de
我 希 望 你 的 **猜 测** 是 正 确 的 。
I hope your **guess** is correct.

71 裁判   cái pàn   **Noun:** referee

yǒu jǐ gè duì yuán zài hé cái pàn zhēng zhí
有 几 个 队 员 在 和 **裁 判** 争 执 。
Several players are arguing with the **referee**.

72 采购   cǎi gòu   **Verb:** to procure; to purchase (in business)
                              Noun: procurement

Verb
wǒ men yào qù yà zhōu cǎi gòu gāng tiě cái liào
我 们 要 去 亚 洲 **采 购** 钢 铁 材 料 。
We are going to Asia to **purchase** steel materials.

Noun
zhè kě yǐ jiāo gěi xīn de cǎi gòu jīng lǐ
这 可 以 交 给 新 的 **采 购** 经 理 。
This can be handed over to the new **procurement** manager.

73 彩票   cǎi piào   **Noun:** lottery ticket

qióng rén bǐ fù rén gèng xǐ huān mǎi cǎi piào
穷 人 比 富 人 更 喜 欢 买 彩 票 。
The poor like to buy **lottery tickets** more than the rich.

74 餐馆   cān guǎn   **Noun:** restaurant

táng rén jiē yǒu jǐ bǎi jiā zhōng cān guǎn
唐 人 街 有 几 百 家 中 餐 馆 。
There are hundreds of Chinese **restaurants** in Chinatown.

75 餐厅   cān tīng   **Noun:** canteen

zhè jiā cān tīng de lǎo bǎn shì dé guó huá rén
这 家 餐 厅 的 老 板 是 德 国 华 人 。
The owner of this **canteen** is German-Chinese.

76 餐饮   cān yǐn   **Noun:** catering; food (service)

zhè jǐ nián cān yǐn yè hé fú wù yè fā zhǎn de hǎo
这 几 年 餐 饮 业 和 服 务 业 发 展 得 好 。
The **catering** and service industries have developed well in recent years.

77 草原   cǎo yuán   **Noun:** grasslands; prairie

wǒ xiǎng qù nèi méng gǔ de cǎo yuán shàng qí mǎ
我 想 去 内 蒙 古 的 草 原 上 骑 马 。
I want to go horse riding on the **grasslands** of Inner Mongolia.

78 册   cè   **Classifier** for book volumes

zhè tào jiào cái yí gòng yǒu liù cè
这 套 教 材 一 共 有 六 册 。
There are six **volumes** in this set of textbooks.

79 层次   céng cì   **Noun:** level; gradation

^{zài} ^{bù} ^{tóng} ^{de} ^{céng} ^{cì} ^{xué} ^{xí} ^{zhòng} ^{diǎn} ^{bù} ^{yí} ^{yàng}
在 不 同 的 **层 次** ，学 习 重 点 不 一 样 。
At different **levels**, the focus of learning is different.

80 叉   chā   **Noun:** cross

^{qǐng} ^{gěi} ^{cuò} ^{de} ^{huà} ^{chā} ^{duì} ^{de} ^{huà} ^{gōu}
请 给 错 的 画 **叉** ，对 的 画 勾 。
Please draw a **cross** the wrong ones and tick the correct ones.

81 叉子   chā zi   **Noun:** fork

^{zhè} ^{lǐ} ^{yǒu} ^{dāo} ^{zi} ^{chā} ^{zi} ^{kuài} ^{zi} ^{hé} ^{pán} ^{zi}
这 里 有 刀 子 、**叉 子** 、筷 子 和 盘 子 。
Here are knives, **forks**, chopsticks and plates.

82 差别   chā bié   **Noun:** difference

^{měi} ^{guó} ^{hé} ^{yīng} ^{guó} ^{de} ^{xī} ^{cān} ^{lǐ} ^{yí} ^{yǒu} ^{chā} ^{bié} ^{ma}
美 国 和 英 国 的 西 餐 礼 仪 有 **差 别** 吗 ？
Are there **differences** in Western food etiquette between the US and the UK?

83 差距   chā jù   **Noun:** disparity

^{zài} ^{shì} ^{yè} ^{shàng} ^{tā} ^{hé} ^{wǒ} ^{de} ^{chā} ^{jù} ^{hěn} ^{dà}
在 事 业 上 ，他 和 我 的 **差 距** 很 大 。
In terms of career, there is a big **disparity** between him and me.

84 插   chā   **Verb:** to insert

^{yóu} ^{guǎn} ^{de} ^{shì} ^{pín} ^{chā} ^{le} ^{tài} ^{duō} ^{guǎng} ^{gào}
油 管 的 视 频 **插** 了 太 多 广 告 。
There are too many ads **inserted** into YouTube videos.

85 查询 chá xún
Verb: to check; to inquire

qǐng wèn, zài nǎ ér kě yǐ **chá xún** wǒ de bāo guǒ
请 问， 在 哪 儿 可 以 **查 询** 我 的 包 裹？
Excuse me, where can I **check** my parcel?

86 差（一）点 chà (yi) diǎn
Adverb: almost; nearly

nà cì chǎo jià ràng wǒ men **chà yi diǎn** fēn shǒu
那 次 吵 架 让 我 们 **差 一 点** 分 手。
That fight **almost** caused us to break up.

87 拆 chāi
Verb: to tear apart; to open (boxes)

shèng dàn jié dāng tiān, hái zi men xǐ huān **chāi** lǐ wù
圣 诞 节 当 天， 孩 子 们 喜 欢 **拆** 礼 物。
On Christmas Day, children love **opening** presents.

88 拆除 chāi chú
Verb: to tear down; to demolish

zhèng fǔ dǎ suàn **chāi chú** zhè xiē wēi fáng
政 府 打 算 **拆 除** 这 些 危 房。
The government plans to **demolish** these dilapidated buildings.

89 产业 chǎn yè
Noun: industry; property

zhuān jiā men xiǎng tiáo zhěng **chǎn yè** jié gòu
专 家 们 想 调 整 **产 业** 结 构。
Experts want to adjust the **industrial** structure.

90 长度 cháng dù
Noun: length

wǒ yào cè liáng kè tīng de **cháng dù** hé kuān dù
我 要 测 量 客 厅 的 **长 度** 和 宽 度。
I need to measure the **length** and width of the living room.

91 长寿 cháng shòu **Adjective:** long life (longevity)

wǒ zhù nǐ shēng rì kuài lè ! jiàn kāng cháng shòu
我 祝 你 生 日 快 乐 ! 健 康 **长 寿** !
I wish you a happy birthday! Enjoy a healthy and **long life**!

92 肠 cháng **Noun:** intestine; bowel

tā shuō zhè dào cài shì zhū cháng zuò de
她 说 这 道 菜 是 猪 **肠** 做 的 。
She said the dish was made from pig **intestines**.

93 尝 cháng **Verb:** to have a taste

kàn shàng qù hěn hǎo chī , nǐ yào cháng ma ?
看 上 去 很 好 吃 , 你 要 **尝** 吗 ?
It looks delicious, do you want **to have a taste**?

94 尝试 cháng shì **Verb:** to attempt / **Noun:** attempt

Verb
tā dǎ suàn cí zhí , rán hòu cháng shì chuàng yè
他 打 算 辞 职 , 然 后 **尝 试** 创 业 。
He plans to quit his job and **attempt** to start a business.

Noun
rú guǒ cháng shì shī bài , tā zài zhǎo xīn gōng zuò
如 果 **尝 试** 失 败 , 他 再 找 新 工 作 。
If the **attempt** fails, he will find a new job again.

95 厂长 chǎng zhǎng **Noun:** factory director/boss

wǒ yuē chǎng zhǎng zài míng yuè fàn diàn tán shēng yì
我 约 **厂 长** 在 明 月 饭 店 谈 生 意 。
I invited the **factory boss** to discuss business at Moon Hotel.

96 场面

chǎng miàn — **Noun:** scene

zhè bù diàn yǐng de qiāng shā chǎng miàn hěn kǒng bù
这 部 电 影 的 枪 杀 **场 面** 很 恐 怖。
The shooting **scenes** in this movie were terrifying.

97 倡导

chàng dǎo — **Verb:** to advocate

kàng yì zhě men chàng dǎo bǎo hù huán jìng
抗 议 者 们 **倡 导** 保 护 环 境。
Protesters **advocate** protecting the environment.

98 超越

chāo yuè — **Verb:** to surpass; to transcend

wáng zǒng jiān de néng lì chāo yuè le duō shù yuán gōng
王 总 监 的 能 力 **超 越** 了 多 数 员 工。
Director Wang's ability **surpasses** that of most employees.

99 车主

chē zhǔ — **Noun:** car owner

chē zi bào zhà hòu chē zhǔ yě shī zōng le
车 子 爆 炸 后，**车 主** 也 失 踪 了。
After the car exploded, the **owner** also disappeared.

100 称

chēng — **Verb:** to call

wǒ men dōu chēng gōng sī de zǒng jīng lǐ zhāng zǒng
我 们 都 **称** 公 司 的 总 经 理 张 总。
We all **call** the company's CEO "Boss Zhang."

101 称号

chēng hào — **Noun:** title

yǒu xiē rén bù xǐ huān zhèng shì de gōng zuò chēng hào
有 些 人 不 喜 欢 正 式 的 工 作 **称 号**。
Some people don't like formal job **titles**.

102 成本   chéng běn   **Noun:** cost (of production)

<small>zhè xiē chǎn pǐn de chéng běn shì měi jiàn yīng bàng</small>
这 些 产 品 的 **成 本** 是 每 件 35 英 镑 。
The **cost** of these products is £35 each.

103 成交   chéng jiāo   **Verb:** to make a deal

<small>xié shāng hòu wǒ men chéng jiāo le dì yī pī dìng dān</small>
协 商 后 ， 我 们 **成 交** 了 第 一 批 订 单 。
After negotiation, we **made a deal** for the first batch of orders.

104 成效   chéng xiào   **Noun:** results; effects

<small>wǒ xī wàng kuài diǎn kàn dào chǎn pǐn de xiāo shòu chéng xiào</small>
我 希 望 快 点 看 到 产 品 的 销 售 **成 效** 。
I hope to see the sales **results** of the product soon.

105 成语   chéng yǔ   **Noun:** idiom

<small>wǒ xǐ huān xué zhōng wén chéng yǔ yòu hǎo wán yòu hǎo yòng</small>
我 喜 欢 学 中 文 **成 语** ， 又 好 玩 又 好 用 。
I like learning Chinese **idioms**, it's fun and useful.

106 承办   chéng bàn   **Verb:** to host/undertake (business activity)

<small>cù xiāo huó dòng shì guǎng gào zhōng jiè chéng bàn de</small>
促 销 活 动 是 广 告 中 介 **承 办** 的 。
Promotional activities are **hosted** by an advertising agency.

107 城里   chéng lǐ   **Noun:** in the city; in town

<small>chéng lǐ de fáng jià bǐ jiāo qū gāo hěn duō</small>
城 里 的 房 价 比 郊 区 高 很 多 。
Housing prices **in the city** are much higher than in the suburbs.

108 乘车   chéng chē   **Verb:** to take bus/car

_{wǒ zài gōng zuò rì děi chéng chē qù shì qū shàng bān}
我 在 工 作 日 得 乘 车 去 市 区 上 班 。
I have **to take a bus** to work in the city on weekdays.

109 乘(坐)   chéng (zuò)   **Verb:** to seat (in a vehicle)

_{zhè liàng miàn bāo chē kě yǐ chéng zuò liù gè rén}
这 辆 面 包 车 可 以 乘 坐 六 个 人 。
The van can **seat** seat six people.

_{wǒ dǎ suàn cóng xī bān yá chéng chuán qù yīng guó}
我 打 算 从 西 班 牙 乘 船 去 英 国 。
I plan **to take** a boat from Spain to the UK.

110 乘客   chéng kè   **Noun:** passenger

_{zāo gāo yǒu yí wèi chéng kè wàng ná xíng li le}
糟 糕 ！ 有 一 位 乘 客 忘 拿 行 李 了 。
Oops! A **passenger** forgot to take his luggage.

111 吃力   chī lì   **Adjective:** laborious

_{duì yú wǒ wài gōng dǎ sǎo fáng jiān hěn chī lì}
对 于 我 外 公 ， 打 扫 房 间 很 吃 力 。
For my grandpa, cleaning the house is **laborious**.

112 池子   chí zi   **Noun:** pond; pool

_{tā de huā yuán yǒu yí zuò qiáo hé yí gè chí zi}
他 的 花 园 有 一 座 桥 和 一 个 池 子 。
His garden has a bridge and a **pond**.

113 迟   chí   **Adjective:** late; delayed

bào qiàn   jiāo tōng tài dǔ   wǒ kě néng huì yǒu diǎn chí
抱 歉， 交 通 太 堵， 我 可 能 会 有 点 **迟**。
Sorry, there's heavy traffic, I might be a little **late**.

114 冲动   chōng dòng   **Verb:** be impulsive
Noun: impulsivity

Verb
tā yòu shēng qì yòu chōng dòng   gāng gāng pǎo chū qù le
他 又 生 气 又 **冲 动**， 刚 刚 跑 出 去 了。
He was angry and **impulsive** and just ran out.

Noun
chōng dòng shì tā de xìng gé quē diǎn
冲 动 是 他 的 性 格 缺 点。
Impulsivity is his character flaw.

115 冲突   chōng tū   **Verb:** to clash
Noun: conflict

Verb
nǐ kàn   jǐng chá zài hé yóu xíng duì wǔ chōng tū
你 看， 警 察 在 和 游 行 队 伍 **冲 突**。
Look, the police is **clashing** with the protest march.

Noun
zhè zhǒng zhèng zhì chōng tū bù róng yì jiě jué
这 种 政 治 **冲 突** 不 容 易 解 决。
This type of political **conflict** is not easy to resolve.

116 充足   chōng zú   **Adjective:** sufficient; adequate

qí shí   tā de cún kuǎn bú suàn chōng zú
其 实， 他 的 存 款 不 算 **充 足**。
In fact, his savings are not considered **sufficient**.

117 愁   chóu   **Verb:** to worry; to be anxious

tā yì zhí chóu mǎi bu qǐ fáng zi
他 一 直 **愁** 买 不 起 房 子。
He always **worries** about not being able to afford a house.

118 丑　　chǒu　　**Adjective:** ugly

tā suī rán yòu pàng yòu chǒu　dàn shì hěn shàn liáng
他 虽 然 又 胖 又 **丑** ， 但 是 很 善 良 。
Although he's fat and **ugly**, he is very kind-hearted.

119 臭　　chòu　　**Adjective:** smelly; stinky

tā yòu qiāo qiāo fàng pì le　zhēn chòu
他 又 悄 悄 放 屁 了 ， 真 **臭** ！
He farted quietly again, so **smelly**!

120 出版　　chū bǎn　　**Verb:** to publish (books and articles)

zhè wèi fǎ guó zuò jiā yǐ jīng chū bǎn le sì shí běn shū
这 位 法 国 作 家 已 经 **出 版** 了 四 十 本 书 。
This French author has **published** forty books.

121 出差　　chū chāi　　**Verb:** to go on a business trip
Noun: business trip

Verb
wǒ xià gè yuè yào chū chāi qù bā lí cǎi fǎng tā
我 下 个 月 要 **出 差** 去 巴 黎 采 访 他 。
I'll **go on a business trip** to Paris next month to interview him.

Noun
wǒ xī wàng zhè cì chū chāi shùn lì
我 希 望 这 次 **出 差** 顺 利 ！
I really hope this **business trip** goes well!

122 出汗　　chū hàn　　**Verb:** to sweat

tā miàn shì de shí hòu tài jǐn zhāng　chū hàn le
她 面 试 的 时 候 太 紧 张 ， **出 汗** 了 。
She was so nervous during the job interview that she **sweated**.

123 出于   chū yú   **Preposition:** out of; proceed from

chū yú lǐ mào, wǒ méi yǒu zhí jiē gào sù tā
出于 礼 貌， 我 没 有 直 接 告 诉 她。
Out of politeness, I didn't tell her directly.

124 初期   chū qī   **Noun:** early stage or days

zài liàn ài chū qī, hěn duō rén dōu yǒu jī qíng
在 恋 爱 **初 期**， 很 多 人 都 有 激 情。
In the **early stages** of a relationship, many people are passionate.

125 除非   chú fēi   **Conjunction:** unless

chú fēi tā dào qiàn, bù rán wǒ bú huì yuán liàng tā
除非 他 道 歉， 不 然 我 不 会 原 谅 他。
Unless he apologizes, (otherwise) I won't forgive him.

126 除夕   chú xī   **Noun:** Lunar New Year's Eve

zài chú xī, wǒ men huì yì qǐ fàng yān huā
在 **除 夕**， 我 们 会 一 起 放 烟 花。
On **Lunar New Year's Eve**, we will set off fireworks together.

127 厨房   chú fáng   **Noun:** kitchen

chú shī men zài chú fáng zuò shēng rì dàn gāo
厨 师 们 在 **厨 房** 做 生 日 蛋 糕。
The chefs are in the **kitchen** making birthday cakes.

128 处罚 chǔ fá
Verb: to punish; to penalize
Noun: punishment

Verb
rú guǒ nǐ nǚ ér fàn cuò， nǐ huì chǔ fá tā ma？
如 果 你 女 儿 犯 错， 你 会 **处 罚** 她 吗？
If your daughter makes a mistake, will you **punish** her?

Noun
zhè děi kàn qíng kuàng， chǔ fá bù yí dìng yǒu xiào
这 得 看 情 况， **处 罚** 不 一 定 有 效。
It depends; **punishments** are not necessarily effective.

129 处分 chǔ fèn
Verb: to discipline
Noun: disciplinary action

Verb
tā yīn wèi huì lù fǎ guān ér bèi chǔ fèn
他 因 为 贿 赂 法 官 而 被 **处 分**。
He was **disciplined** for bribing a judge.

Noun
dà jiā duì zhè cì de chǔ fèn méi yǒu yì yì
大 家 对 这 次 的 **处 分** 没 有 异 议。
Everyone has no objection to this **disciplinary action**.

130 处在 chǔ zài
Verb: to be at (situations)

nǐ xiàn zài chǔ zài shì yè de diān fēng， gǎn jué rú hé
你 现 在 **处 在** 事 业 的 巅 峰，感 觉 如 何？
You are now **at** the peak of your career, how do you feel?

131 传达 chuán dá
Verb: to convey; to pass on (information)

qǐng bǎ zǒng cái de zhǐ shì chuán dá gěi dài biǎo tuán
请 把 总 裁 的 指 示 **传 达** 给 代 表 团。
Please **convey** the CEO's instructions to the delegation.

132 传递 chuán dì
Verb: to deliver; to transmit

kuài dì yuán fù zé chuán dì xìn jiàn hé bāo guǒ
快 递 员 负 责 **传 递** 信 件 和 包 裹。
Couriers are responsible for **delivering** letters and packages.

133 传真　　　chuán zhēn　　**Noun:** fax

fā chuán zhēn shì bu shì yǒu diǎn guò shí
发 传 真 是 不 是 有 点 过 时 ？
Is sending a **fax** a bit outdated?

134 窗帘　　　chuāng lián　　**Noun:** curtain (of window)

wǒ hěn xǐ huān bái sè de léi sī chuāng lián
我 很 喜 欢 白 色 的 蕾 丝 窗 帘 。
I like the white lace **curtains** very much.

135 闯　　　chuǎng　　**Verb:** to rush (to places)

shén me ？ yǒu rén chuǎng jìn le huà zhuāng jiān
什 么 ？ 有 人 闯 进 了 化 妆 间 ？
What? Someone **rushed** into the dressing room?

136 创立　　　chuàng lì　　**Verb:** to establish; to found

zhè sān wèi chuàng shǐ rén zài qù nián chuàng lì le gōng sī
这 三 位 创 始 人 在 去 年 创 立 了 公 司 。
The three founders **founded** the company last year.

137 辞典　　　cí diǎn　　**Noun:** encyclopedia

wǒ de shū fáng yǒu yì běn chéng yǔ hé yàn yǔ cí diǎn
我 的 书 房 有 一 本 成 语 和 谚 语 辞 典 。
There is an idiom and proverb **encyclopedia** in my study room.

138 辞职　　cí zhí

Verb: to resign
Noun: resignation

Verb

wǒ zhǔn bèi xià zhōu xiàng jīng lǐ zhèng shì cí zhí
我 准 备 下 周 向 经 理 正 式 **辞 职**。
I am planning to formally **resign** to my manager next week.

Noun

jiē xià lái wǒ yào xiě yì fēng cí zhí xìn
接 下 来， 我 要 写 一 封 **辞 职** 信。
Next, I need to write a **resignation** letter.

139 此后　　cǐ hòu

Conjunction: from now on; after that

cǐ hòu wǒ huì zhuān xīn chéng lì zì jǐ de gōng sī
此 后， 我 会 专 心 成 立 自 己 的 公 司。
From now on, I will focus on setting up my own company.

140 此刻　　cǐ kè

Noun: now; at this moment

wǒ hěn gāo xìng nǐ cǐ kè yǒu rú cǐ jiān dìng de jué xīn
我 很 高 兴 你 **此 刻** 有 如 此 坚 定 的 决 心。
I'm glad you have such firm determination **at this moment**.

141 此时　　cǐ shí

Noun: now; at this time

wǒ huì jì zhù nǐ cǐ shí zuò de chéng nuò
我 会 记 住 你 **此 时** 做 的 承 诺。
I will remember the promise you made **at this time**.

142 聪明　　cōng míng

Adjective: smart; clever

tā yǐ qián yǒu diǎn yú chǔn xiàn zài hěn cōng míng
他 以 前 有 点 愚 蠢， 现 在 很 **聪 明**。
He was a bit stupid before, now he's **smart**.

143 从而   cóng ér   **Conjunction:** thus; thereby

tā měi tiān liàn xí, cóng ér tí gāo le zhōng wén kǒu yǔ
他 每 天 练 习，**从 而** 提 高 了 中 文 口 语。
He practiced every day, **thereby** improved his spoken Chinese.

144 从中   cóng zhōng   **Adverb:** out of; therefrom

zhè cì shī bài ràng tā cóng zhōng xué dào le jiào xùn
这 次 失 败 让 他 **从 中** 学 到 了 教 训。
He learned a lesson **out of** this failure.

145 脆   cuì   **Adjective:** crispy; brittle; clear voice

shǔ tiáo yòu cuì yòu hǎo chī, dàn bú jiàn kāng
薯 条 又 **脆** 又 好 吃，但 不 健 康。
French fries are **crispy** and tasty, but not healthy.

146 存款   cún kuǎn   **Noun:** bank savings

zì cóng zhǎng gōng zī hòu, wǒ de cún kuǎn yě duō le
自 从 涨 工 资 后，我 的 **存 款** 也 多 了。
Since the salary increase, I also have more **savings**.

147 寸   cùn   **Measurement:** Chinese inch (3⅓ cm)

zhè gè xiǎo huā píng dà gài sān cùn gāo
这 个 小 花 瓶 大 概 三 **寸** 高。
This small vase is about three **inches** tall.

148 达成   dá chéng   **Verb:** to reach (agreement)

xī wàng tā men néng jǐn kuài dá chéng xié yì
希 望 他 们 能 尽 快 **达 成** 协 议。
Hopefully they can **reach** an agreement soon.

149 答   dá   **Verb:** to answer; to respond

zhè dào tí zhǐ yǒu lǐ hóng dá duì
这 道 题 只 有 李 红 **答** 对 。
Only Li Hong **answered** this question correctly.

150 答复   dá fù   **Verb:** to reply   **Noun:** reply

Verb
wǒ huì kǎo lǜ yi xià   míng tiān dá fù nǐ
我 会 考 虑 一 下 ， 明 天 **答 复** 你 。
I'll consider it a bit and **reply** to you tomorrow.

Noun
yǐ jīng liǎng tiān le   wǒ hái shì méi shōu dào tā de dá fù
已 经 两 天 了 ， 我 还 是 没 收 到 他 的 **答 复** 。
It's 2 days and I still haven't received his **reply**.

151 打   dǎ   **Verb:** to hit; to beat   **Preposition:** from; since

Verb
shén me tā zài jiē shàng bèi liú máng dǎ le
什 么 ？ 他 在 街 上 被 流 氓 **打** 了 ？
What? He was **beaten** by gangsters on the street?

Pre.
dǎ nà tiān qǐ   tā wǎn shàng zài yě bù chū qù le
打 那 天 起 ， 他 晚 上 再 也 不 出 去 了 。
From that day on, he never went out at night again.

152 打扮   dǎ ban   **Verb:** to dress up

jīn tiān de wǎn huì shàng   tā dǎ ban de hěn piào liang
今 天 的 晚 会 上 ， 她 **打 扮** 得 很 漂 亮 。
At today's party, she **dressed up** beautifully.

153 打包   dǎ bāo   **Verb:** to pack

kuài dǎ bāo xíng li   zán men míng zǎo liù diǎn chū fā
快 **打 包** 行 李 ， 咱 们 明 早 六 点 出 发 。
Quickly **pack** your bags, we'll leave at 6am tomorrow.

154 打击   dǎ jī

Verb: to strike; to crack down
Noun: blow (difficulty)

Verb
打击 犯 罪 是 警 察 的 职 责 。
dǎ jī fàn zuì shì jǐng chá de zhí zé
Cracking down on crime is the duty of the police.

Noun
她 受 不 了 离 婚 的 **打击** ， 天 天 哭 。
tā shòu bu liǎo lí hūn de dǎ jī tiān tiān kū
She couldn't bear the **blow** of the divorce, crying every day.

155 打架   dǎ jià

Verb: to fight (physical)

我 的 狗 又 和 我 的 猫 **打架** 了 。
wǒ de gǒu yòu hé wǒ de māo dǎ jià le
My dog **fought** with my cat again.

156 打扰   dǎ rǎo

Verb: to disturb

小 声 点 ， 不 要 **打扰** 孩 子 睡 觉 。
xiǎo shēng diǎn bú yào dǎ rǎo hái zi shuì jiào
Keep your voice down, don't **disturb** the childrens' sleep.

157 大胆   dà dǎn

Adjective: bold; daring

他 想 尝 试 跳 伞 ？ 真 **大胆** ！
tā xiǎng cháng shì tiào sǎn zhēn dà dǎn
He wants to try skydiving? How **bold**!

158 大都   dà dōu

Adverb: mostly; for the most part

我 的 朋 友 **大都** 是 胆 小 鬼 。
wǒ de péng yǒu dà dōu shì dǎn xiǎo guǐ
My friends are **mostly** cowards.

159 大纲   dà gāng   **Noun:** outline; compendium

wǒ zài cǎo nǐ shì chǎng yíng xiāo dà gāng
我 在 草 拟 市 场 营 销 **大 纲**。
I'm drafting a marketing plan **outline**.

160 大伙   dà huǒ   **Pronoun:** you; all; everybody (colloquial)

dà huǒ yǒu shén me yì jiàn   suí shí gào sù wǒ
大 伙 有 什 么 意 见， 随 时 告 诉 我。
If **you** have any suggestions, tell me anytime.

161 大奖赛   dà jiǎng sài   **Noun:** grand prix

tā zài dà jiǎng sài zhōng huò dé le dì yī míng
他 在 **大 奖 赛** 中 获 得 了 第 一 名。
He finished first in the **Grand Prix**.

162 大脑   dà nǎo   **Noun:** brain; cerebrum

rén de dà nǎo shén jīng zǔ zhī fēi cháng fù zá
人 的 **大 脑** 神 经 组 织 非 常 复 杂。
The neural tissue of the human **brain** is very complex.

163 大事   dà shì   **Noun:** big event

bì yè diǎn lǐ shì dà shì wǒ dāng rán yào cān jiā
毕 业 典 礼 是 **大 事**， 我 当 然 要 参 加。
The graduation ceremony is a **big event**, of course I will attend.

164 大厅   dà tīng   **Noun:** hall; lobby

duì bù qǐ nín bu néng zài dà tīng lǐ chōu yān
对 不 起， 您 不 能 在 **大 厅** 里 抽 烟。
Sorry, you can't smoke in the **lobby**.

165 大象   dà xiàng   **Noun:** elephant

dòng wù yuán dōng biān yǒu dà xiàng hé shī zi
动 物 园 东 边 有 **大 象** 和 狮 子 。
There are **elephants** and lions on the east side of the zoo.

166 大熊猫   dà xióng māo   **Noun:** giant panda

dà xióng māo bèi chēng wéi hé píng dà shǐ
大 熊 猫 被 称 为 和 平 大 使 。
Giant pandas are called ambassadors of peace.

167 大于   dà yú   more than

tā de shēn jià dà yú shí yì měi yuán
他 的 身 价 **大 于** 十 亿 美 元 。
His net worth is **more than** a billion dollars.

168 大致   dà zhì   **Adverb:** roughly

tā míng xià de gōng sī dà zhì yǒu jiǔ gè
他 名 下 的 公 司 **大 致** 有 九 个 。
There are **roughly** nine companies under his name.

169 呆   dāi   **Verb:** to stay (short time) **Adjective:** dull; slow-witted

Verb
tā men zài tú shū guǎn dāi le liǎng gè xiǎo shí
他 们 在 图 书 馆 **呆** 了 两 个 小 时 。
They **stayed** in the library for two hours.

Adj.
tā kàn shàng qù yǒu diǎn dāi dàn qí shí hěn jiǎo huá
他 看 上 去 有 点 **呆** ， 但 其 实 很 狡 猾 。
He looks a little **dull**, but actually very cunning.

170 待   dāi   **Verb:** to stay (long time)

chū yù hòu， tā yì zhí dāi zài jiā zhōu
出 狱 后， 他 一 直 **待** 在 加 州。
After being released from prison, he **stayed** in California.

171 代价   dài jià   **Noun:** cost/price (of sacrifice)

wèi le jiù hái zi， tā fù chū le shēng mìng de dài jià
为 了 救 孩 子， 他 付 出 了 生 命 的 **代价**。
In order to save the child, he paid the **price** with his life.

172 代理   dài lǐ   **Verb:** to act on behalf of (formal)   **Noun:** agent

Verb
lǜ shī huì dài lǐ zhāng xiān shēng qiān zì
律 师 会 **代理** 张 先 生 签 字。
The lawyer will sign **on behalf of** Mr. Zhang.

Noun
tā céng shì gōng sī ōu zhōu shì chǎng de dài lǐ
他 曾 是 公 司 欧 洲 市 场 的 **代理**。
He used to be the company's European market **agent**.

173 带有   dài yǒu   **Verb:** to imply; to bring

zhè tiáo shì pín nèi róng hǎo xiàng dài yǒu xìng qí shì
这 条 视 频 内 容 好 像 **带 有** 性 歧 视。
The content of this video seems **to imply** sexism.

174 贷款   dài kuǎn   **Verb:** take out a loan   **Noun:** loan

Verb
wèi le mǎi fáng， wǒ men xiàng yín háng dài kuǎn le
为 了 买 房， 我 们 向 银 行 **贷款** 了。
In order to buy a house, we **took out a loan** from the bank.

Noun
xiàn zài měi gè yuè yào huán liǎng qiān yīng bàng de dài kuǎn
现 在 每 个 月 要 还 两 千 英 镑 的 **贷款**。
Now I have to repay a **loan** at £2000 per month.

175 单一   dān yī

Adjective: plain; simple; sole (singular)

zhè jiàn xī zhuāng de shè jì yǒu diǎn dān yī
这 件 西 装 的 设 计 有 点 单 一 。
The design of this suit is a bit **plain**.

176 胆   dǎn

Noun: gut; gallbladder

tīng shuō háng tiān yuán men dōu hěn dǎn dà
听 说 航 天 员 们 都 很 胆 大 。
I heard that astronauts are very brave (**gut** big).

177 胆小   dǎn xiǎo

Adjective: timid; cowardly

wǒ de gǒu dǎn xiǎo bù gǎn guò qiáo
我 的 狗 胆 小 ， 不 敢 过 桥 。
My dog is too **timid** to cross the bridge.

178 蛋糕   dàn gāo

Noun: cake

wǒ jiě gěi wǒ zuò le yí gè qiǎo kè lì dàn gāo
我 姐 给 我 做 了 一 个 巧 克 力 蛋 糕 。
My older sister made me a chocolate **cake**.

179 当场   dāng chǎng

Adverb: on the spot

shén me ？ tā dāng chǎng xiàng nǐ xià guì qiú hūn le
什 么 ？ 他 当 场 向 你 下 跪 求 婚 了 ？
What? He knelt down and proposed to you **on the spot**?

180 当代   dāng dài

Noun: contemporary; current time

shén me shì yǐng xiǎng dāng dài zuì dà de fā míng
什 么 是 影 响 当 代 最 大 的 发 明 ？
What's the most influential invention of the **current time**?

181 当年　　dāng nián　　**Noun:** in those years

dāng nián wǒ men jié hūn de shí hòu, tā cái 23 suì
当年我们结婚的时候，她才23岁。
In those years when we got married, she was only 23.

182 当前　　dāng qián　　**Noun:** currently; at present

zhè shì wǒ men dāng qián de shǒu yào rèn wù
这 是 我 们 **当 前** 的 首 要 任 务 。
This is our top priority **at present**.

183 当选　　dāng xuǎn　　**Verb:** to be elected

tā gāng gāng dāng xuǎn le měi guó de fù zǒng tǒng
她 刚 刚 **当 选** 了 美 国 的 副 总 统 。
She just got **elected** as Vice President of the USA.

184 挡　　dǎng　　**Verb:** to block

yǒu xiē kàng yì zhě zài qián miàn dǎng lù
有 些 抗 议 者 在 前 面 **挡** 路 。
Some protesters are **blocking** the road ahead.

185 到来　　dào lái　　**Noun:** arrival

hái zi men hěn qī dài shèng dàn lǎo rén de dào lái
孩 子 们 很 期 待 圣 诞 老 人 的 **到 来** 。
Kids are looking forward to **arrival** of Father Christmas.

186 倒是　　dào shì　　**Adverb:** actually (contrarily)

wǒ shì chéng rén, duì jié rì dào shì wú suǒ wèi
我 是 成 人 ， 对 节 日 **倒 是** 无 所 谓 。
I'm an adult, **actually** don't care about festivals.

187 道德　　dào dé　　**Noun:** morality; moral

nǐ tīng shuō guò dào dé bǎng jià ma
你 听 说 过 **道 德** 绑 架 吗 ？
Have you ever heard of **moral** coercion?

188 得了　　dé le　　**Phrase:** stop it; hold it (colloquial)

dé le zhè zhǒng tǎo lùn zhēn de yǒu yì yì ma
得 了 ！ 这 种 讨 论 真 的 有 意 义 吗 ？
Hold it! Is this type of discussion really meaningful?

189 得以　　dé yǐ　　**Verb:** be able to (formal)

shuāng fāng de wèn tí hé shí cái néng dé yǐ jiě jué
双 方 的 问 题 何 时 才 能 **得 以** 解 决 ？
When will the issues of both parties **be able to** be resolved?

190 等候　　děng hòu　　**Verb:** to wait (formal)

shì bīng men zài děng hòu jiāng jūn de mìng lìng
士 兵 们 在 **等 候** 将 军 的 命 令 。
The soldiers are **waiting** for the general's orders.

191 等级　　děng jí　　**Noun:** grade; rank; ranking

tā shì zǒng sī lìng děng jí zuì gāo
他 是 总 司 令 ， **等 级** 最 高 。
He is the Commander-in-Chief, the highest **rank**.

192 低于　　dī yú　　under; lower than

tā de míng shēng hé dì wèi bù dī yú rèn hé rén
他 的 名 声 和 地 位 不 **低 于** 任 何 人 。
His reputation and status are not **lower than** anyone.

193 地带   dì dài   **Noun:** area; district

<small>zhè gè dì dài tài cháo shī, bú shì hé zhā yíng</small>
这个**地带**太潮湿，不适合扎营。
This **area** is too wet for camping.

194 地形   dì xíng   **Noun:** terrain

<small>kē xué jiā men hái zài kǎo chá dì xíng</small>
科学家们还在考察**地形**。
Scientists are still examining the **terrain**.

195 地震   dì zhèn   **Noun:** earthquake

<small>tā men fā xiàn, zhè lǐ yǒu pín fán de dì zhèn</small>
他们发现，这里有频繁的**地震**。
They discovered that there are frequent **earthquakes** here.

196 递   dì   **Verb:** to pass; to hand

<small>má fán nǐ bǎ shǒu jī dì gěi wǒ</small>
麻烦你把手机**递**给我。
May I trouble you **to hand** me the phone.

197 递给   dì gěi   **Verb:** to pass to; to hand over to

<small>yǒu gè tóng shì gāng gāng dì gěi le tā yì zhāng zhǐ tiáo</small>
有个同事刚刚**递给**了他一张纸条。
A colleague had just **handed over** a note **to** him.

198 典礼   diǎn lǐ   **Noun:** ceremony

<small>tā men zài shàng hǎi jǔ bàn le shèng dà de dìng hūn diǎn lǐ</small>
他们在上海举办了盛大的订婚**典礼**。
They held a grand engagement **ceremony** in Shanghai.

199 点燃   diǎn rán   **Verb:** to light; to ignite

nǐ kàn, ào yùn huǒ jù bèi diǎn rán le
你看，奥运火炬被**点燃**了！
Look, the Olympic torch is **lit**!

200 电池   diàn chí   **Noun:** battery

wǒ yào mǎi xīn de diàn chí hé chōng diàn qì
我要买新的**电池**和充电器。
I need to buy new **batteries** and chargers.

201 电饭锅   diàn fàn guō   **Noun:** rice cooker

zhè kǒu diàn fàn guō shì péng yǒu sòng wǒ de lǐ wù
这口**电饭锅**是朋友送我的礼物。
This **rice cooker** was a gift from a friend.

202 电子版   diàn zǐ bǎn   **Noun:** digital version/ edition

nǐ gèng xǐ huān yòng diàn zǐ bǎn hái shì zhǐ zhì bǎn
你更喜欢用**电子版**还是纸质版？
Do you prefer to use an **digital edition** or printed edition?

203 调动   diào dòng   **Verb:** to muster; to mobilize (army or forces)

zhèng fǔ diào dòng le yì bǎi míng jǐng chá zhèn yā yóu xíng
政府**调动**了一百名警察镇压游行。
The government **mobilized** 100 policemen to suppress the protest.

204 丢   diū   **Verb:** to lose; to throw away

wǒ de qián bāo diū le bāng wǒ zhǎo yi zhǎo
我的钱包**丢**了，帮我找一找。
I've **lost** my wallet, help me find it.

205 动机   dòng jī   **Noun:** motive; purpose

nǐ xiāng xìn tā， bìng qīng chǔ tā de **dòng jī** ma？
你 相 信 他， 并 清 楚 他 的 **动 机** 吗 ？
Do you trust him and understand his **motives**?

206 动手   dòng shǒu   **Verb:** to act; to start

shí jiān jǐn jí， wǒ děi kuài diǎn **dòng shǒu**。
时 间 紧 急， 我 得 快 点 **动 手** 。
Time is urgent, I have **to act** quickly.

207 动态   dòng tài   **Noun:** dynamic; motion; trends

zhuān jiā men zài fēn xī jīng jì **dòng tài**。
专 家 们 在 分 析 经 济 **动 态** 。
Experts are analyzing economic **trends**.

208 动员   dòng yuán   **Verb:** to mobilize (staff or people) **Noun:** mobilization

Verb
wǒ men yào xiǎng bàn fǎ **dòng yuán** dà jiā de jī jí xìng。
我 们 要 想 办 法 **动 员** 大 家 的 积 极 性 。
We must find ways **to mobilize** everyone's enthusiasm.

Noun
gǎn xiè nǐ men cān jiā zhè cì **dòng yuán** huì。
感 谢 你 们 参 加 这 次 **动 员** 会 。
Thank you for participating in this **mobilization** meeting.

209 冻   dòng   **Verb:** to freeze

chē zi bèi bīng **dòng** le， wǒ yào mǎ shàng jiě **dòng**。
车 子 被 冰 **冻** 了， 我 要 马 上 解 冻 。
The car is **frozen** by ice; I need to thaw it immediately.

210 洞   dòng   **Noun:** hole; cave

shén me ？ tā yí gè rén zhù zài shān dòng
什 么 ？ 她 一 个 人 住 在 山 洞 ？
What? She lives alone in a mountain **cave**?

211 豆制品   dòu zhì pǐn   **Noun:** bean products

hěn duō sù shí zhě hěn xǐ huān chī dòu zhì pǐn
很 多 素 食 者 很 喜 欢 吃 豆 制 品 。
Many vegetarians like to eat **bean products**.

212 毒   dú   **Noun:** poison; toxin

tā yīn wèi xī dú bèi zhuā le
他 因 为 吸 毒 被 抓 了 。
He was arrested for taking drugs (**poison**).

213 堆   duī   **Verb:** to build (pile up)   **Classifier** for a piles or stacks

Verb
hái zi men zài wài miàn duī xuě rén
孩 子 们 在 外 面 堆 雪 人 。
The children are **building** snowmen outside.

Noun
wǒ zài bāng tā zhěng lǐ yì duī wén jiàn
我 在 帮 她 整 理 一 堆 文 件 。
I'm helping her to organize a **pile of** documents.

214 对立   duì lì   **Verb:** to oppose

kě xī ， tā de zhèng zhì lì chǎng hé wǒ de duì lì
可 惜 ， 他 的 政 治 立 场 和 我 的 对 立 。
Unfortunately, his political stance **opposes** to mine.

215 对应　　duì yìng　　**Adjective:** corresponding

tā men zhèng zài xún zhǎo duì yìng de jiě jué fāng àn
他 们 正 在 寻 找 **对 应** 的 解 决 方 案 。

They are looking for a **corresponding** solution (approach to solving the problem).

216 吨　　dūn　　**Measurement:** tonne (1000 kilograms)

kǎ chē shàng zhuāng le yì dūn qì yóu
卡 车 上 装 了 一 **吨** 汽 油 。

The truck is loaded with a **tonne** of gasoline.

217 朵　　duǒ　　**Classifier** for flowers and clouds

zài qíng rén jié， tā sòng le wǒ 99 duǒ fěn méi guī
在 情 人 节 ， 他 送 了 我 99 **朵** 粉 玫 瑰 。

On Valentine's Day, he gifted me 99 pink roses.

218 躲　　duǒ　　**Verb:** to hide; to avoid; to dodge

dāng shí tā bù hǎo yì si de duǒ zài qiáng hòu
当 时 他 不 好 意 思 地 **躲** 在 墙 后 。

At that time, he embarrassedly **hid** behind the wall.

219 儿女　　ér nǚ　　**Noun:** children (sons and daughters)

zhè gè lǎo rén de ér nǚ dōu zài guó wài dìng jū
这 个 老 人 的 **儿 女** 都 在 国 外 定 居 。

The old man's **children** all settled abroad.

220 耳朵　　ěr duo　　**Noun:** ear

wǒ xǐ huān mō wǒ de gǒu de dà ěr duo
我 喜 欢 摸 我 的 狗 的 大 **耳 朵** 。

I love to stroke my dog's big **ears**.

221 二维码

èr wéi mǎ

Noun: QR code

sǎo miáo zhè gè èr wéi mǎ jiù kě yǐ fù kuǎn
扫 描 这 个 **二 维 码** 就 可 以 付 款 。
You can just scan this **QR code** to pay.

222 发布

fā bù

Verb: to post;
to release

wǒ zuì xǐ huān de bó zhǔ měi zhōu wǔ fā bù shì pín
我 最 喜 欢 的 博 主 每 周 五 **发 布** 视 频 。
My favorite blogger **posts** a video every Friday.

223 发觉

fā jué

Verb: to realize

wǒ men dōu fā jué tā kě néng huái yùn le
我 们 都 **发 觉** 她 可 能 怀 孕 了 。
We all **realized** that she might be pregnant.

224 发射

fā shè

Verb: to launch
(rocket)

nǐ cān guān guò huǒ jiàn fā shè jī dì ma
你 参 观 过 火 箭 **发 射** 基 地 吗 ？
Have you ever visited a rocket **launch** site?

225 发行

fā xíng

Verb: to issue

zhōng yāng yín háng zhǔn bèi fā xíng xīn de huò bì
中 央 银 行 准 备 **发 行** 新 的 货 币 。
Central banks are preparing **to issue** new currency.

226 罚

fá

Verb: to punish;
to fine; to penalize

yīn wèi jiǔ jià tā bèi fá le wǔ bǎi měi yuán
因 为 酒 驾 ， 他 被 **罚** 了 五 百 美 元 。
Due to drunk driving, he was **fined** $500.

227 罚款   fá kuǎn   **Verb:** to impose a fine/forfeit
Noun: fine; forfeit

Verb
^{qí} 其 ^{shí} 实 ， ^{zhè} 这 ^{shì} 是 ^{tā} 他 ^{dì} 第 ^{yī} 一 ^{cì} 次 ^{bèi} 被 ^{jǐng} 警 ^{chá} 察 **罚款** 。
In fact, this is the first time he was **fined** by the police.

Noun
^{zhè} 这 ^{cì} 次 **罚款** ^{gěi} 给 ^{le} 了 ^{tā} 他 ^{hěn} 很 ^{dà} 大 ^{de} 的 ^{jiào} 教 ^{xùn} 训 。
This **fine** taught him a big lesson.

228 法规   fǎ guī   **Noun:** rule of law; statute

^{xìng} 幸 ^{kuī} 亏 ^{duō} 多 ^{shù} 数 ^{rén} 人 ^{zūn} 遵 ^{shǒu} 守 ^{jiāo} 交 ^{tōng} 通 **法规** 。
Fortunately, most people obey traffic **rules**.

229 法制   fǎ zhì   **Noun:** legal system

^{wán} 完 ^{shàn} 善 **法制** ^{shì} 是 ^{jiàn} 建 ^{lì} 立 ^{hé} 和 ^{xié} 谐 ^{shè} 社 ^{huì} 会 ^{de} 的 ^{jī} 基 ^{chǔ} 础 。
Improving the **legal system** is the basis for building a harmonious society.

230 繁荣   fán róng   **Adjective:** booming; prosperous
Noun: boom; prosperity

Adj.
^{zhè} 这 ^{xiàng} 项 ^{gǎi} 改 ^{gé} 革 ^{ràng} 让 ^{jīng} 经 ^{jì} 济 **繁荣** 。
This reform made the economy **prosperous**.

Noun
^{dà} 大 ^{jiā} 家 ^{xī} 希 ^{wàng} 望 ^{wéi} 维 ^{chí} 持 **繁荣** ^{yǔ} 与 ^{hé} 和 ^{píng} 平 。
Everyone hopes to maintain **prosperity** and peace.

231 返回　　　　fǎn huí　　　　**Verb:** to return; to go back

退 休 后 ， 他 **返 回** 了 家 乡 。
tuì xiū hòu，tā fǎn huí le jiā xiāng
After retirement, he **returned** to his hometown.

232 防治　　　　fáng zhì　　　　**Verb:** to prevent and control

他 们 在 做 **防 治** 森 林 火 灾 的 工 作 。
tā men zài zuò fáng zhì sēn lín huǒ zāi de gōng zuò
They are working **to prevent and control** forest fire.

233 放大　　　　fàng dà　　　　**Verb:** to zoom; to magnify

她 敏 感 ， 总 是 **放 大** 小 问 题 。
tā mǐn gǎn，zǒng shì fàng dà xiǎo wèn tí
She is sensitive and always **magnifies** small problems.

234 放弃　　　　fàng qì　　　　**Verb:** to give up

虽 然 有 困 难 ， 但 是 我 不 会 **放 弃** 。
suī rán yǒu kùn nán，dàn shì wǒ bú huì fàng qì
Although there are difficulties, I will not **give up**.

235 分成　　　　fēn chéng　　　　**Verb:** to divide into

请 帮 我 把 蛋 糕 **分 成** 十 块 。
qǐng bāng wǒ bǎ dàn gāo fēn chéng shí kuài
Please help me **divide** the cake **into** ten pieces.

236 分解　　　　fēn jiě　　　　**Verb:** to dissect; to decompose

张 医 生 在 教 学 员 **分 解** 身 体 。
zhāng yī shēng zài jiāo xué yuán fēn jiě shēn tǐ
Dr. Zhang is instructing trainees on how **to dissect** the body.

237 分类   fēn lèi   **Verb:** to classify; to assort

qǐng àn zhào zhǒng lèi bǎ zhè xiē shū jí fēn lèi
请 按 照 种 类 把 这 些 书 籍 **分 类**。
Please **classify** these books by category.

238 分离   fēn lí   **Verb:** to part; to separate; to detach

fēn lí wǔ nián hòu tā zhōng yú jiàn dào le ér zi
分 离 五 年 后， 她 终 于 见 到 了 儿 子。
After **separating** for 5 years, she finally saw her son.

239 分析   fēn xī   **Verb:** to analyze   **Noun:** analysis

Verb
zī xún shī zài wèi kè hù fēn xī wèn tí
咨 询 师 在 为 客 户 **分 析** 问 题。
The consultant is **analyzing** the problem for the client .

Noun
zhè shì jù tǐ de fēn xī bào gào
这 是 具 体 的 **分 析** 报 告。
This is a detailed **analysis** report.

240 分享   fēn xiǎng   **Verb:** to share (joy, right, experience)

tóng xué men xiāng hù fēn xiǎng le liú xué jīng yàn
同 学 们 相 互 **分 享** 了 留 学 经 验。
Classmates **shared** their overseas study experiences with each other.

241 丰收   fēng shōu   **Noun:** harvest

zhōng qiū jié hé gǎn ēn jié dōu shì fēng shōu de jié rì
中 秋 节 和 感 恩 节 都 是 **丰 收** 的 节 日。
Mid-Autumn Festival and Thanksgiving are both **harvest** festivals.

242 风度　　fēng dù　　**Noun:** demeanor

wǒ de wèi hūn fū yòu shuài yòu yǒu fēng dù
我 的 未 婚 夫 又 帅 又 有 **风 度** ！
My fiancé is handsome and has a good **demeanor**!

243 风光　　fēng guāng　　**Adjective:** grand
Noun: scenery

Adj.
tā chéng nuò huì gěi wǒ yí gè fēng guāng de hūn lǐ
他 承 诺 会 给 我 一 个 **风 光** 的 婚 礼 。
He promised to give me a **grand** wedding.

Noun
háng zhōu xī hú de fēng guāng hěn měi
杭 州 西 湖 的 **风 光** 很 美 。
The **scenery** of West Lake in Hangzhou is beautiful.

244 封　　fēng　　**Verb:** to seal; to block
Noun: envelopes

Verb
zāo gāo lù bèi fēng le wǒ men děi diào tóu
糟 糕 ！ 路 被 **封** 了 ， 我 们 得 掉 头 。
Oops! the road is **blocked**, we have to turn around.

Noun
wǒ mǎi le yì bāo zhōng guó gǔ diǎn xìn fēng
我 买 了 一 包 中 国 古 典 信 **封** 。
I bought a pack of classical Chinese letter **envelopes**.

245 疯(狂)　　fēng (kuáng)　　**Adjective:** mad; crazy; insane

tā měi zhōu gōng zuò gè xiǎo shí tài fēng le
他 每 周 工 作 70 个 小 时 ？ 太 **疯** 了 ！
He works 70 hours a week? That's **mad**!

tā bèi chēng wéi lì shǐ shàng zuì fēng kuáng de zǒng tǒng
他 被 称 为 历 史 上 最 **疯 狂** 的 总 统 。
He was called the craziest (most **crazy**) president in history.

246 扶   fú

Verb: to hold (for support)

tā de jiǎo shòu shāng le, wǒ yào fú tā zǒu
他 的 脚 受 伤 了， 我 要 **扶** 他 走。

His foot is injured, I have to (**hold** him) help him walk.

247 服从   fú cóng

Verb: to obey
Noun: obedience

Verb
xià shǔ bì xū fú cóng shàng sī de mìng lìng ma
下 属 必 须 **服 从** 上 司 的 命 令 吗？

Do subordinates have **to obey** orders from their superiors?

Noun
fú cóng bìng bú dài biǎo zhōng chéng
服 从 并 不 代 表 忠 诚！

Obedience actually does not mean loyalty!

248 幅   fú

Classifier for pictures and images

wǒ de shū fáng yǒu yì fú zhōng guó shān shuǐ huà
我 的 书 房 有 一 **幅** 中 国 山 水 画。

There is a Chinese landscape painting in my study.

249 幅度   fú dù

Noun: range; magnitude

xiāo shòu liàng de fú dù hé wǒ yù qī de bù yí yàng
销 售 量 的 **幅 度** 和 我 预 期 的 不 一 样。

The **magnitude** of sales is different to my expectation.

250 福利   fú lì

Noun: welfare; material benefit

bú shì měi gè rén dōu kě yǐ shēn qǐng fú lì
不 是 每 个 人 都 可 以 申 请 **福 利**。

Not everyone can apply for **welfare**.

251 辅助   fǔ zhù

Verb: to assist (study or work)
Noun: assistance

Verb

wǒ qǐng le jiā jiào **fǔ zhù** nǚ ér de shù xué
我 请 了 家 教 **辅 助** 女 儿 的 数 学 。
I hired a tutor **to assist** my daughter with math.

Noun

yǒu le **fǔ zhù** tā jìn bù de hěn kuài
有 了 **辅 助** ， 她 进 步 得 很 快 。
With **assistance**, she made rapid progress.

252 负责人   fù zé rén

Noun: head (person in charge)

lǎo wáng shì shì chǎng bù mén de **fù zé rén**
老 王 是 市 场 部 门 的 **负 责 人** 。
Wang is the **head** of the marketing department.

253 附件   fù jiàn

Noun: attachment (file)

wǒ de jiǎn lì zài **fù jiàn** lǐ qǐng nín chá kàn
我 的 简 历 在 **附 件** 里 ， 请 您 查 看 。
My resume is in the **attachment**, please take a look.

254 改革   gǎi gé

Verb: to reform
Noun: reform

Verb

wǒ men zhōu de yī liáo tǐ xì xū yào **gǎi gé**
我 们 州 的 医 疗 体 系 需 要 **改 革** 。
Our state's health care system needs **to be reformed**.

Noun

zhōu zhǎng gāng gāng fā bù le **gǎi gé** fāng àn
州 长 刚 刚 发 布 了 **改 革** 方 案 。
The governor just released a **reform** scheme.

255 干脆   gān cuì

Adverb: simply; frankly

bié yóu yù qǐng **gàn cuì** de huí dá
别 犹 豫 ， 请 **干 脆** 地 回 答 。
Don't hesitate, please answer **frankly**.

256 干扰 gān rǎo **Verb:** to disrupt

gōng chǎng de zào yīn gān rǎo le jū mín de shēng huó
工厂的噪音**干扰**了居民的生活。
The noise from the factory **disrupted** residents' lives.

257 干预 gān yù **Verb:** to intervene; to interfere

jūn zhǔ méi yǒu quán lì gān yù zhèng fǔ de xíng zhèng
君主没有权力**干预**政府的行政。
The monarch has no power to **interfere** with the administration of the government.

258 感想 gǎn xiǎng **Noun:** thoughts; reflections

nǐ duì zhè jiàn shì de gǎn xiǎng shì shén me
你对这件事的**感想**是什么？
What are your **thoughts** on this matter?

259 钢笔 gāng bǐ **Noun:** fountain pen

wǒ yé ye shōu cáng le yì zhī chún jīn de gāng bǐ
我爷爷收藏了一支纯金的**钢笔**。
My grandfather collected a solid gold **fountain pen**.

260 钢琴 gāng qín **Noun:** piano

wǒ zài wéi yě nà jiàn guò zhè wèi gāng qín dà shī
我在维也纳见过这位**钢琴**大师。
I met this **piano** master in Vienna.

261 高大 gāo dà **Adjective:** lofty; tall and big

jiào liàn shēn cái gāo dà jī ròu fā dá
教练身材**高大**，肌肉发达。
The coach is **tall and big**, and has great muscles.

262 高度　　　　　gāo dù　　　**Noun:** altitude; height

wǒ yào cè liáng tā de cháng dù kuān dù hé gāo dù
我 要 测 量 它 的 长 度 、 宽 度 和 **高 度** 。
I need to measure its length, width and **height**.

263 高跟鞋　　　gāo gēn xié　　**Noun:** high heels (shoes)

wǒ wǎng gòu le yì shuāng bái sè de gāo gēn xié
我 网 购 了 一 双 白 色 的 **高 跟 鞋** 。
I bought a pair of white **high heels** online.

264 高温　　　　gāo wēn　　　**Noun:** high temperature

wǒ shòu de liǎo dī wēn dàn shòu bu liǎo gāo wēn
我 受 得 了 低 温 ， 但 受 不 了 **高 温** 。
I can bear low temperatures, but not **high temperatures**.

265 高于　　　　gāo yú　　　**Verb:** to be above; to be higher than

tā de nián shōu rù gāo yú píng jūn shuǐ píng
他 的 年 收 入 **高 于** 平 均 水 平 。
His annual income is **above** the average level.

266 高原　　　　gāo yuán　　　**Noun:** plateau; highland

wǒ bú tài xí guàn zhè lǐ de gāo yuán qì hòu
我 不 太 习 惯 这 里 的 **高 原** 气 候 。
I'm not used to the climate of the **highland** here.

267 搞　　　　　gǎo　　　**Verb:** to get; to do (colloquial)

zài shì yè shàng gǎo guān xi yǒu diǎn fù zá
在 事 业 上 ， **搞** 关 系 有 点 复 杂 。
In career, **getting** connections is a bit complicated.

268 搞好 gǎo hǎo **Verb:** to be good/ do well (work or relationships)

hé tóng shì men gǎo hǎo guān xi hěn zhòng yào
和 同 事 们 **搞 好** 关 系 很 重 要。
It is important to **build good** relationships with colleagues.

269 歌(曲) gē (qǔ) **Noun:** song

zhè shǒu gē tīng shàng qù hěn shú xi
这 首 **歌** 听 上 去 很 熟 悉。
This **song** sounds familiar.

270 隔壁 gé bì **Noun:** next door

dāng rán le gé bì de lín jū zǒng shì chàng tā
当 然 了, **隔 壁** 的 邻 居 总 是 唱 它。
Of course, the **next door** neighbor always sings it.

271 个儿 gè'r **Noun:** height; stature

tā gè 'r xiǎo suǒ yǐ ǒu ěr bèi qī fù
他 **个 儿** 小, 所 以 偶 尔 被 欺 负。
His **stature** is small, so was bullied occasionally.

272 跟前 gēn qián **Noun:** in front of

bǎ tā dài dào wǒ gēn qián ràng wǒ kàn kan
把 他 带 到 我 **跟 前** 让 我 看 看。
Bring him over (**in front**) to me to have a look.

273 跟(随) gēn (suí) **Verb:** to follow; to come with

hǎo de tā míng tiān huì gēn suí fù mǔ lái
好 的, 他 明 天 会 **跟 随** 父 母 来。
Okay, he will **come with** his parents tomorrow.

274 更换   gēng huàn   **Verb:** to change (for replacement)

wǒ zuì jìn zài kǎo lǜ gēng huàn zhí wèi
我 最 近 在 考 虑 **更 换** 职 位 。
Recently I've been considering **changing** job positions.

275 更新   gēng xīn   **Verb:** to update; to renew

zhè gè ruǎn jiàn dà gài měi nián gēng xīn yí cì
这 个 软 件 大 概 每 年 **更 新** 一 次 。
This software is **updated** approximately once a year.

276 工艺   gōng yì   **Noun:** craft (product)

zhè jiàn gōng yì pǐn de zhì liàng hé shè jì dōu hǎo
这 件 **工 艺** 品 的 质 量 和 设 计 都 好 。
The quality and design of this **craft** product are both good.

277 工作日   gōng zuò rì   **Noun:** workday; working day

zài gōng zuò rì wǒ yì bān méi shí jiān shè jiāo
在 **工 作 日** ， 我 一 般 没 时 间 社 交 。
During the **workday**, I generally don't have time to socialize.

278 公告   gōng gào   **Noun:** public notice; announcement

nǐ kàn dào gōng sī jīn tiān fā bù de gōng gào le ma
你 看 到 公 司 今 天 发 布 的 **公 告** 了 吗 ？
Did you see the **announcement** the company made today?

279 公认   gōng rèn   **Verb:** to acknowledge; to recognize (publicly)

tā shì guó jì shàng gōng rèn de rén dào zhǔ yì zhě
他 是 国 际 上 **公 认** 的 人 道 主 义 者 。
He is an internationally **recognized** humanitarian.

280 公式　gōng shì　**Noun:** formula

zhè shì jīng jì xué jiā shǐ yòng de gōng xū gōng shì
这是经济学家使用的供需**公式**。
This is the **formula** of supply and demand used by economists.

281 公正　gōng zhèng　**Adjective:** fair; just; impartial

wǒ jué de fǎ yuàn de pàn jué gōng zhèng
我觉得法院的判决**公正**。
I think the court's decision is **fair**.

282 共计　gòng jì　**Verb:** to sum; to total

péi cháng jīn gòng jì jiǔ shí wǔ wàn měi yuán
赔偿金**共计**九十五万美元。
The damage cost **totaled** $950,000.

283 共享　gòng xiǎng　**Verb:** to share/enjoy together

tīng shuō nà duì shuāng bāo tāi gòng xiǎng yí gè nán péng yǒu
听说那对双胞胎**共享**一个男朋友。
I heard that the twins **share** one boyfriend **together**.

284 沟　gōu　**Noun:** ditch; gully

zāo gāo chē lún xiàn rù gōu lǐ le
糟糕！车轮陷入**沟**里了。
Oops! The wheel got stuck in the **ditch**.

285 沟通   gōu tōng

Verb: to communicate (interpersonal)
Noun: communication

Verb
tā wú fǎ gēn qián qī shēn rù de gōu tōng
他 无 法 跟 前 妻 深 入 地 **沟 通** 。
He was unable **to communicate** deeply with his ex-wife.

Noun
gōu tōng wèn tí shì tā men lí hūn de yuán yīn
沟 通 问 题 是 他 们 离 婚 的 原 因 。
Communication problems were the reason for their divorce.

286 估计   gū jì

Verb: to estimate
Noun: estimation

Verb
wǒ gū jì zhè zuò qiáo yǒu qiān nián de lì shǐ
我 **估 计** 这 座 桥 有 千 年 的 历 史 。
I **estimate** this bridge is thousands of years old.

Noun
nǐ de gū jì shì zhèng què de zhēn lì hài
你 的 **估 计** 是 正 确 的 ， 真 厉 害 ！
Your **estimation** is correct, so awesome!

287 古老   gǔ lǎo

Adjective: ancient; age-old

wǒ zhī dào yí gè guān yú tā de gǔ lǎo chuán shuō
我 知 道 一 个 关 于 它 的 **古 老** 传 说 。
I know an **ancient** legend about it.

288 鼓   gǔ

Noun: drum

yǒu rén zài wǔ shī dǎ gǔ
有 人 在 舞 狮 、 打 **鼓** 。
Some people are doing the lion dance and playing **drums**.

289 鼓励   gǔ lì

Verb: to encourage
Noun: encouragement

Verb
tā yì zhí gǔ lì wǒ zhuī qiú mèng xiǎng
她 一 直 **鼓 励** 我 追 求 梦 想 。
She always **encouraged** me to pursue my dreams.

Noun
wǒ hěn gǎn jī yǒu tā de gǔ lì hé zhī chí
我 很 感 激 有 她 的 **鼓 励** 和 支 持 。
I'm grateful to have her **encouragement** and support.

290 鼓掌   gǔ zhǎng

Verb: to applaud

guān zhòng men dōu zài dà shēng de gǔ zhǎng
观 众 们 都 在 大 声 地 **鼓 掌** 。
The audience is all **applauding** loudly.

291 顾问   gù wèn

Noun: adviser;
consultant

zhè shì xīn lái de jiào yù gù wèn jiào chén yún
这 是 新 来 的 教 育 **顾 问** ， 叫 陈 云 。
This is the new education **consultant** named Chen Yun.

292 怪   guài

Verb: to blame
Adjective: strange

Verb
tā suī rán fàn cuò le dàn shì lǎo bǎn méi guài tā
她 虽 然 犯 错 了 ， 但 是 老 板 没 **怪** 她 。
Although she made a mistake, the boss didn't **blame** her.

Adj.
zhè bú guài bì jìng tā men shì dì xià qíng rén
这 不 **怪** ， 毕 竟 他 们 是 地 下 情 人 。
This is not **strange**, after all they're secret lovers.

293 关怀   guān huái

Noun: care/concern
(formal)

gū ér yuàn hěn gǎn xiè nín de juān zèng hé guān huái
孤 儿 院 很 感 谢 您 的 捐 赠 和 **关 怀** 。
The orphanage is grateful for your donations and **care**.

294 关键   guān jiàn   **Noun:** key (crux)
Adjective: crucial; critical

Noun

chéng gōng de guān jiàn zài yú bú xiè de nǔ lì
成 功 的 **关 键** 在 于 不 懈 的 努 力 。
The **key** to success lies in relentless effort.

Adj.

zài zhè guān jiàn shí kè   nǐ yào zhuā jǐn shí jiān
在 这 **关 键** 时 刻 , 你 要 抓 紧 时 间 。
At this **critical** moment, you need to hurry up.

295 冠军   guàn jūn   **Noun:** champion

zhè cì bǐ sài de guàn jūn hé yà jūn shì shéi
这 次 比 赛 的 **冠 军** 和 亚 军 是 谁 ?
Who are the **champions** and the runners-up of this competition?

296 光荣   guāng róng   **Noun:** glory; honor
Adjective: honored; glorious

Noun

dāng tuán duì lǐng dǎo shì yì zhǒng guāng róng
当 团 队 领 导 是 一 种 **光 荣** 。
Being a team leader is a type of **honor**.

Adj.

néng wèi dà jiā fú wù ràng wǒ gǎn jué guāng róng
能 为 大 家 服 务 让 我 感 觉 **光 荣** 。
It makes me feel **honored** to be able to serve you all.

297 光线   guāng xiàn   **Noun:** light

wǒ de fáng jiān xiàng nán   suǒ yǐ guāng xiàn hǎo
我 的 房 间 向 南 , 所 以 **光 线** 好 。
My room faces south, so it has good **light**.

298 广   guǎng   **Adjective:** far; broad; vast

tā jīng yàn fēng fù jiàn shí guǎng
她 经 验 丰 富 , 见 识 **广** 。
She's richly experienced and has **far** vision.

299 广泛　　guǎng fàn

Adjective: extensive; wide-ranging

tā men gōng sī de yè wù fàn wéi guǎng fàn
他们公司的业务范围**广泛**。
Their company's business scope is **extensive**.

300 规划　　guī huà

Verb: to plan (strategically)
Noun: plan

Verb
wǒ men zài guī huà xīn de zhù fáng jī dì
我们在**规划**新的住房基地。
We are **planning** new housing sites.

Noun
guī huà fāng àn yǐ jīng bèi pī zhǔn le
规划方案已经被批准了。
The **plan** (scheme) has been approved.

301 鬼　　guǐ

Noun: ghost; dirty trick

tiān a zhè shì shén me guǐ
天啊！这是什么**鬼**？
Oh my god! What the heck (**ghost**) is this?

302 柜子　　guì zi

Noun: cupboard; cabinet

wǒ ér zi kěn dìng cáng zài guì zi lǐ le
我儿子肯定藏在**柜子**里了。
My son must be hiding in the **cupboard**.

303 滚　　gǔn

Verb: to roll
Phrase: get lost; piss off

Verb
xiǎo gǒu men zài cǎo dì shàng gǔn lái gǔn qù
小狗们在草地上**滚**来**滚**去。
The puppies are **rolling** back and forth on the grass.

Phrase
shén me tā mà nǐ hái ràng nǐ gǔn
什么！他骂你，还让你**滚**？
What! He scolded you and told you to **get lost**?

304 锅　　　guō　　　**Noun:** pot

zhè kǒu tiě guō suī rán chǒu　dàn hěn yǒu yòng
这 口 铁 **锅** 虽 然 丑 ， 但 很 有 用 。
Although this iron **pot** is ugly, it is very useful.

305 国籍　　　guó jí　　　**Noun:** nationality; citizenship

tīng shuō tā yǒu měi guó hé fǎ guó de shuāng chóng guó jí
听 说 他 有 美 国 和 法 国 的 双 重 **国 籍** 。
I heard that he has dual **citizenship** of the U.S. and France.

306 国民　　　guó mín　　　**Noun:** citizen; national

jūn duì de rèn wù shì bǎo hù guó mín de ān quán
军 队 的 任 务 是 保 护 **国 民** 的 安 全 。
The mission of the military is to protect the safety of **citizens**.

307 过度　　　guò dù　　　**Adjective:** overdone; excessive
Adverb: excessively

Adj.
guò dù xī yān duì shēn tǐ de shāng hài hěn dà
过 度 吸 烟 对 身 体 的 伤 害 很 大 。
Over-smoking is very harmful to the body.

Adv.
tā jiā bān guò dù　gǎn jué yā lì shān dà
他 加 班 **过 度** ， 感 觉 压 力 山 大 。
He works overtime **excessively** and felt stressed out.

308 过敏　　　guò mǐn　　　**Adjective:** allergic

wǒ de yí gè tóng shì duì huā shēng guò mǐn
我 的 一 个 同 事 对 花 生 **过 敏** 。
One of my colleagues is **allergic** to peanuts.

309 过于 guò yú **Adverb:** too much (negative)

<ruby>不<rt>bú</rt></ruby> <ruby>要<rt>yào</rt></ruby> <ruby>过<rt>guò</rt></ruby> <ruby>于<rt>yú</rt></ruby> <ruby>担<rt>dān</rt></ruby> <ruby>心<rt>xīn</rt></ruby>，<ruby>没<rt>méi</rt></ruby> <ruby>那<rt>nà</rt></ruby> <ruby>么<rt>me</rt></ruby> <ruby>严<rt>yán</rt></ruby> <ruby>重<rt>zhòng</rt></ruby>。

Don't worry **too much**, it's not that serious.

310 害 hài **Verb:** to harm; to hurt

<ruby>放<rt>fàng</rt></ruby> <ruby>心<rt>xīn</rt></ruby>，<ruby>他<rt>tā</rt></ruby> <ruby>只<rt>zhǐ</rt></ruby> <ruby>会<rt>huì</rt></ruby> <ruby>保<rt>bǎo</rt></ruby> <ruby>护<rt>hù</rt></ruby> <ruby>你<rt>nǐ</rt></ruby>，<ruby>不<rt>bú</rt></ruby> <ruby>会<rt>huì</rt></ruby> <ruby>害<rt>hài</rt></ruby> <ruby>你<rt>nǐ</rt></ruby>。

Don't worry, he will only protect you; not **harm** you.

311 汗 hàn **Noun:** sweat

<ruby>他<rt>tā</rt></ruby> <ruby>被<rt>bèi</rt></ruby> <ruby>吓<rt>xià</rt></ruby> <ruby>得<rt>de</rt></ruby> <ruby>出<rt>chū</rt></ruby> <ruby>汗<rt>hàn</rt></ruby> <ruby>了<rt>le</rt></ruby>。

He was so scared that he sweated (out **sweat**).

312 好运 hǎo yùn **Noun:** good luck

<ruby>祝<rt>zhù</rt></ruby> <ruby>你<rt>nǐ</rt></ruby> <ruby>好<rt>hǎo</rt></ruby> <ruby>运<rt>yùn</rt></ruby>！<ruby>我<rt>wǒ</rt></ruby> <ruby>会<rt>huì</rt></ruby> <ruby>想<rt>xiǎng</rt></ruby> <ruby>你<rt>nǐ</rt></ruby> <ruby>的<rt>de</rt></ruby>。

Wish you **good luck**! I will miss you.

313 号召 hào zhào **Verb:** to call upon

<ruby>候<rt>hòu</rt></ruby> <ruby>选<rt>xuǎn</rt></ruby> <ruby>人<rt>rén</rt></ruby> <ruby>在<rt>zài</rt></ruby> <ruby>号<rt>hào</rt></ruby> <ruby>召<rt>zhào</rt></ruby> <ruby>群<rt>qún</rt></ruby> <ruby>众<rt>zhòng</rt></ruby> <ruby>为<rt>wèi</rt></ruby> <ruby>他<rt>tā</rt></ruby> <ruby>投<rt>tóu</rt></ruby> <ruby>票<rt>piào</rt></ruby>。

The candidate is **calling** upon the masses to vote for him.

314 合并 hé bìng **Verb:** to merge

<ruby>我<rt>wǒ</rt></ruby> <ruby>们<rt>men</rt></ruby> <ruby>的<rt>de</rt></ruby> <ruby>两<rt>liǎng</rt></ruby> <ruby>个<rt>gè</rt></ruby> <ruby>部<rt>bù</rt></ruby> <ruby>门<rt>mén</rt></ruby> <ruby>最<rt>zuì</rt></ruby> <ruby>近<rt>jìn</rt></ruby> <ruby>被<rt>bèi</rt></ruby> <ruby>合<rt>hé</rt></ruby> <ruby>并<rt>bìng</rt></ruby> <ruby>了<rt>le</rt></ruby>。

Our two departments were recently **merged**.

315 合成   hé chéng   **Verb:** to synthesize
Noun: synthesis

Verb

tā men yòng rén gōng zhì néng hé chéng le zhè zhāng tú
他 们 用 人 工 智 能 **合 成** 了 这 张 图 。
They used artificial intelligence **to synthesize** this image.

Noun

zhè shì yì zhǒng xiān jìn de hé chéng jì shù
这 是 一 种 先 进 的 **合 成** 技 术 。
This is an advanced **synthesis** technology.

316 盒   hé   **Classifier** for small boxes or containers

tā sòng gěi le wǒ yì hé jīng měi de qiǎo kè lì
他 送 给 了 我 一 **盒** 精 美 的 巧 克 力 。
He gave me **a box of** exquisite chocolates.

317 盒(子)   hé (zi)   **Noun:** case; small box

zhè gè bāo zhuāng hé zi què shí fēi cháng yōu yǎ
这 个 包 装 **盒 子** 确 实 非 常 优 雅 。
This packaging **case** is indeed very elegant.

318 盒饭   hé fàn   **Noun:** packed meal; boxed lunch

dǎo yǎn hé yǎn yuán men zài pái duì lǐng hé fàn
导 演 和 演 员 们 在 排 队 领 **盒 饭** 。
The directors and actors are queuing up to get **boxed lunches**.

319 贺卡   hè kǎ   **Noun:** greeting card

zhè shì wǒ shè jì de chūn jié hè kǎ
这 是 我 设 计 的 春 节 **贺 卡** 。
This is the Spring Festival **greeting card** I designed.

320 恨　hèn　**Verb:** to hate　**Noun:** hatred

Verb
fēn shǒu hòu　tā hèn guò qián nán yǒu yí duàn shí jiān
分手后，她 **恨** 过前男友一段时间。
After the breakup, she **hated** her ex-boyfriend for a while.

Noun
ài hé hèn dōu shì fù zá de gǎn qíng
爱和 **恨** 都是复杂的感情。
Love and **hatred** are both complex emotions.

321 猴　hóu　**Noun:** monkey

nǐ zhī dào měi hóu wáng sūn wù kōng de gù shì ma
你知道美 **猴** 王孙悟空的故事吗？
Do you know the story of Sun Wukong, the **Monkey** King?

322 后悔　hòu huǐ　**Verb:** to regret

qí shí　wǒ fēi cháng hòu huǐ gēn tā hé zuò
其实，我非常 **后悔** 跟他合作。
In fact, I very much **regret** cooperating with him.

323 胡同　hú tong　**Noun:** alley; bystreet

wǒ wài pó de jiā zài běi jīng de yí gè hú tong
我外婆的家在北京的一个 **胡同**。
My grandmother's home is in a Beijing **alley**.

324 胡子　hú zi　**Noun:** mustache; beard

tā xǐ huān nǐ wài gōng de cháng hú zi ma
她喜欢你外公的长 **胡子** 吗？
Does she like your grandpa's long **beard**?

325 虎 　　　　hǔ 　　　　**Noun:** tiger

nǐ kàn guò diàn yǐng 《 wò hǔ cáng lóng 》 ma ?
你 看 过 电 影 《卧 虎 藏 龙》 吗 ?
Have you seen the movie "Crouching **Tiger**, Hidden Dragon"?

326 华语 　　　　huá yǔ 　　　　**Noun:**
Chinese language

zài guó wài de huá rén dà duō shù huì shuō huá yǔ
在 国 外 的 华 人 大 多 数 会 说 华 语 。
Most overseas Chinese can speak **Chinese language**.

327 滑 　　　　huá 　　　　**Adjective:** slippery

dì shàng yǒu diǎn huá , qǐng dà jiā xiǎo xīn
地 上 有 点 滑 ， 请 大 家 小 心 。
The ground is a bit **slippery**, so please be careful.

328 化石 　　　　huà shí 　　　　**Noun:** fossil

wǒ yào dài hái zi qù kàn kǒng lóng huà shí
我 要 带 孩 子 去 看 恐 龙 化 石 。
I want to take my kids to see the dinosaur **fossils**.

329 划分 　　　　huà fēn 　　　　**Verb:** to divide

bó wù guǎn bèi huà fēn chéng le bā gè yóu lǎn qū yù
博 物 馆 被 划 分 成 了 八 个 游 览 区 域 。
The museum is **divided** into eight tourist areas.

330 画面 　　　　huà miàn 　　　　**Noun:** scene; frame

jìn mén shí wǒ men bèi yǎn qián de huà miàn mí zhù le
进 门 时 ， 我 们 被 眼 前 的 画 面 迷 住 了 。
Upon entering, we were fascinated by the **scene** in front.

331 环节　huán jié　**Noun:** session; segment

bú guò, wǒ men cuò guò le dǎo yóu de jiě shuō huán jié
不过，我们错过了导游的解说**环节**。
However, we missed the tour guide's explanation **session**.

332 慌　huāng　**Verb:** to panic; to be in a hurry
Adjective: panicked

Verb
bié huāng, zhè gè shí hòu yí dìng yào lěng jìng
别**慌**，这个时候一定要冷静！
Don't **panic**, you must stay calm at this time!

Adj.
tā kàn shàng qù hěn huāng, wǒ děi ān wèi tā
她看上去很**慌**，我得安慰她。
She looks **panicked**; I have to comfort her.

333 慌忙　huāng máng　**Adverb:** hurriedly

zhǔ chí rén shuō cuò hòu, huāng máng dào qiàn
主持人说错后，**慌忙**道歉。
After the host misspoke, he **hurriedly** apologized.

334 灰色　huī sè　**Adjective:** gray

wǒ de wò shì yǒu yí kuài huī sè de dì tǎn
我的卧室有一块**灰色**的地毯。
I have a **gray** carpet in my bedroom.

335 恢复　huī fù　**Verb:** to recover; **Noun:** recovery

Verb
bié dān xīn, tā de shāng kǒu hěn kuài jiù huì huī fù
别担心，她的伤口很快就会**恢复**。
Don't worry, her wound will **recover** soon

Noun
zhè píng yào kě yǐ jiā sù huī fù
这瓶药可以加速**恢复**。
This bottle of medicine can speed up **recovery**.

336 回报   huí bào

Verb: to repay (out of gratitude)
Noun: repayment; return

Verb
nǐ jué de wǒ men yīng gāi zěn yàng huí bào fù mǔ
你 觉 得 我 们 应 该 怎 样 **回 报** 父 母 ？
How do you think we should **repay** our parents?

Noun
duō péi tā men shì hǎo de huí bào fāng shì
多 陪 他 们 是 好 的 **回 报** 方 式 。
Spending more time with them is a good **repayment** method.

337 回避   huí bì

Verb: to avoid; to dodge

zhèng kè men zǒng shì huí bì mǐn gǎn de wèn tí
政 客 们 总 是 **回 避** 敏 感 的 问 题 。
Politicians always **avoid** sensitive questions.

338 回顾   huí gù

Verb: to look back (for reflection)

huí gù guò qù kě yǐ ràng wǒ men xī qǔ jiào xùn
回 顾 过 去 可 以 让 我 们 吸 取 教 训 。
Looking back at the past allows us to learn lessons.

339 回收   huí shōu

Verb: to recycle

huí shōu bō li píng hé sù liào píng dōu zhòng yào
回 收 玻 璃 瓶 和 塑 料 瓶 都 重 要 。
It's important **to recycle** both glass and plastic bottles.

340 回头   huí tóu

Verb: to turn back; turn one's head
Noun: later

Verb
jì rán zuò le jué dìng jiù bú yào huí tóu
既 然 做 了 决 定 ， 就 不 要 **回 头** 。
Since you've made a decision, don't **look back**.

Noun
zài jiàn wǒ huí tóu gěi nǐ dǎ diàn huà
再 见 ！ 我 **回 头** 给 你 打 电 话 。
Goodbye! I'll call you **later**.

341 回信　huí xìn
Verb: to reply/respond (letter or message)
Noun: reply; response

Verb
dōu yǐ jīng yì zhōu le, tā hái shì méi huí xìn
都 已 经 一 周 了 ， 她 还 是 没 回 信 。
It's been a week and she still hasn't **replied**.

Noun
qí shí, tā de huí xìn sù dù yì zhí dōu màn
其 实 ， 她 的 回 信 速 度 一 直 都 慢 。
In fact, her **response** speed has always been slow.

342 回忆　huí yì
Verb: to recall
Noun: memory; recollection

Verb
wǒ wú fǎ huí yì tā dāng shí shuō de huà
我 无 法 回 忆 他 当 时 说 的 话 。
I'm unable **to recall** what he said at the time.

Noun
nà xiē huí yì zǎo jiù dàn le
那 些 回 忆 早 就 淡 了 。
Those **memories** have long since faded.

343 汇款　huì kuǎn
Verb: to remit money
Noun: remittance

Verb
wǒ yòng wēi xìn gěi tā huì kuǎn le sān bǎi yuán
我 用 微 信 给 他 汇 款 了 三 百 元 。
I **remitted** ¥300 to him using WeChat.

Noun
bǎo liú huì kuǎn jì lù hěn zhòng yào
保 留 汇 款 记 录 很 重 要 。
It is important to keep records of **remittances**.

344 会谈　huì tán
Noun: talk; negotiations (formal)

zhè jiàn yī fú bú shì hé shāng wù huì tán
这 件 衣 服 不 适 合 商 务 会 谈 。
These clothes are not suitable for business **talks**.

345 活力   huó lì   **Noun:** energy; vigor

wǒ de gǒu cái liǎng suì   fēi cháng yǒu huó lì
我的狗才两岁，非常有**活力**。
My dog is only 2 years old and very energetic (have **energy**).

346 活泼   huó pō   **Adjective:** lively (person)

wǒ nǚ ér yòu cōng míng yòu huó pō
我女儿又聪明又**活泼**！
My daughter is so smart and **lively**!

347 火柴   huǒ chái   **Noun:** match (fire)

wǒ jiā yǒu dǎ huǒ jī   dàn méi huǒ chái
我家有打火机，但没**火柴**。
I have a lighter at home, but no **matches**.

348 火腿   huǒ tuǐ   **Noun:** ham

zhè hé huǒ tuǐ yǐ jīng guò qī le   bù néng chī
这盒**火腿**已经过期了，不能吃。
This box of **ham** has expired and cannot be eaten.

349 火灾   huǒ zāi   **Noun:** fire disaster

sēn lín huǒ zāi zào chéng le hěn dà de sǔn shī
森林**火灾**造成了很大的损失。
Forest **fire disasters** caused a lot of damage.

350 或(是)

huò (shì)

Conjunction: or (for statements)

xuǎn zé shì qù fàn guǎn， huò shì qù jiǔ ba
选 择 是 去 饭 馆， **或 是** 去 酒 吧。
The choice is to go to a restaurant **or** go to a bar.

jīn nián huò míng nián jié hūn， wǒ dōu méi yì jiàn
今 年 **或** 明 年 结 婚， 我 都 没 意 见。
Getting married this year **or** next, I have no objection.

351 机器人

jī qì rén

Noun: robot

zhè gè gāo jí jī qì rén yǒu zì jǐ de hù zhào
这 个 高 级 **机 器 人** 有 自 己 的 护 照。
This advanced **robot** has its own passport.

352 机制

jī zhì

Noun: mechanism; machine-made

zhèng fǔ zài zhì dìng xīn de fú lì jī zhì
政 府 在 制 定 新 的 福 利 **机 制**。
The government is developing a new welfare **mechanism**.

353 肌肉

jī ròu

Noun: muscle

tā yǒu jī ròu， kàn shàng qù xìng gǎn
他 有 **肌 肉**， 看 上 去 性 感。
He has **muscles** and looks sexy.

354 基地

jī dì

Noun: base (physical location)

jì zhě qù diàn yǐng pāi shè jī dì cǎi fǎng tā le
记 者 去 电 影 拍 摄 **基 地** 采 访 他 了。
The reporter went to the film set (shooting **base**) to interview him.

355 基金

jī jīn   **Noun:** fund

wǒ men wèi hái zi shè lì le jiào yù jī jīn
我 们 为 孩 子 设 立 了 教 育 基 金 。

We set up an education **fund** for our children.

356 即使

jí shǐ   **Conjunction:** even if

jí shǐ quē qián　wǒ men yě bù néng dòng tā
即 使 缺 钱 ， 我 们 也 不 能 动 它 。

Even if we are short of money, we cannot touch it.

357 集团

jí tuán   **Noun:** group (of company)

zhè shì wǒ men jí tuán de dǒng shì zhǎng lǐ xiān shēng
这 是 我 们 集 团 的 董 事 长 李 先 生 。

This is Mr. Li, the chairman of our **group**.

358 挤

jǐ   **Verb:** to squeeze; to push
Adjective: crowded

Verb

nǐ men xū yào wǒ bāng máng jǐ niú nǎi ma
你 们 需 要 我 帮 忙 挤 牛 奶 吗 ？

Do you need me to help **squeeze** the milk?

Adj.

bú yòng le zhè lǐ gòu jǐ le
不 用 了 ！ 这 里 够 挤 了 。

No need! It's **crowded** enough here.

359 记忆

jì yì   **Noun:** memory

lǎo nián chī dāi zhèng ràng tā shī qù le yì xiē jì yì
老 年 痴 呆 症 让 她 失 去 了 一 些 记 忆 。

Alzheimer's disease has caused her to lose some **memories**.

360 技能　　jì néng　　**Noun:** technical skill

zhè gè xīn de chéng xù yuán yǒu hěn qiáng de jì néng
这 个 新 的 程 序 员 有 很 强 的 **技 能** 。
This new programmer has strong **technical skills**.

361 继承　　jì chéng　　**Verb:** to inherit (good things)

tā qù shì hòu zhí nǚ jì chéng le suǒ yǒu de cái chǎn
他 去 世 后 ，侄 女 **继 承** 了 所 有 的 财 产 。
After his death, his niece **inherited** all the wealth.

362 加热　　jiā rè　　**Verb:** to heat up

wēi bō lú zài nǎ wǒ yào jiā rè fàn cài
微 波 炉 在 哪 ？ 我 要 **加 热** 饭 菜 。
Where is the microwave? I want **to heat up** the meal.

363 加上　　jiā shàng　　**Verb:** plus; to add up;

wǒ men jiā shàng tā men yí gòng jiù bā gè rén
我 们 **加 上** 他 们 ， 一 共 就 八 个 人 。
We **add** them **up** them, in total eight people.

364 加速　　jiā sù　　**Verb:** to speed up; to accelerate

quán qiú nuǎn huà jiā sù le bīng chuān róng huà
全 球 暖 化 **加 速** 了 冰 川 溶 化 。
Global warming has **accelerated** the melting of glaciers.

365 加以　　jiā yǐ　　**Conjunction:** moreover; in addition

zhè gè shì jiàn jiā yǐ qí tā wèn tí dōu hěn ràng rén dān yōu
这 个 事 件 **加 以** 其 他 问 题 ， 都 很 让 人 担 忧 。
This matter **in addition** to other issues are all worrying.

366 夹　　jiā

Verb: to pick up (small objects)
Noun: clip; folder

Verb
nǐ néng yòng kuài zi jiā cài ma
你 能 用 筷 子 **夹** 菜 吗 ？
Can you use chopsticks **to pick up** food?

Noun
wǒ gěi tā mǎi le yí duì hú dié fà jiā
我 给 她 买 了 一 对 蝴 蝶 发 **夹** 。
I bought her a pair of butterfly hair **clips**.

367 甲　　jiǎ

Noun: nail; shell; first (place, grade, rank)

tā qù měi jiǎ diàn xiū zhǐ jiǎ le
她 去 美 **甲** 店 修 指 **甲** 了 。
She went to the **nail** salon to get her **nails** done.

zài zhè cì bǐ sài zhōng xiǎo lǐ dé le jiǎ děng
在 这 次 比 赛 中 ,小 李 得 了 **甲** 等 。
In this competition, Xiaoli won the **first** place.

368 价　　jià

Noun: price/value (use with other words)

zhè kuǎn shǒu jī zhōng yú jiàng jià le
这 款 手 机 终 于 **降 价** 了 。
This **price** of the phone has finally **decreased**.

369 驾驶　　jià shǐ

Verb: to drive

nǐ gǎn zuò wú rén jià shǐ de chū zū chē ma
你 敢 坐 无 人 **驾 驶** 的 出 租 车 吗 ？
Do you dare to take a driverless (nobody **drive**) taxi?

370 驾照　　jià zhào

Noun: driving license

wǒ suì de shí hòu jiù huò dé le jià zhào
我 17 岁 的 时 候 就 获 得 了 **驾 照** 。
I already obtained my **driving license** when I was 17.

371 坚定 — jiān dìng — **Adjective:** firm; steadfast

jiǔ nián lái , wǒ men de ài yì zhí hěn jiān dìng
九 年 来 , 我 们 的 爱 一 直 很 **坚 定** 。
For nine years our love has remained **steadfast**.

372 肩 — jiān — **Noun:** shoulder

qǐng nǐ bāng wǒ cè yí xià jiān kuān hé yāo wéi
请 你 帮 我 测 一 下 **肩** 宽 和 腰 围 。
Please help me measure my **shoulder** width and waistline.

373 艰苦 — jiān kǔ — **Adjective:** tough; bitter (work or life)

shēng huó jiān kǔ de shí hòu , yào bǎo chí lè guān
生 活 **艰 苦** 的 时 候 , 要 保 持 乐 观 。
When life is **tough**, we need to stay optimistic.

374 艰难 — jiān nán — **Adjective:** difficult

chuàng yè shì yì tiáo jiān nán de lù
创 业 是 一 条 **艰 难** 的 路 。
Starting a business is a **difficult** journey.

375 检验 — jiǎn yàn — **Verb:** to inspect (troubleshooting) **Noun:** test inspection

Verb
gōng zuò rén yuán zài jiǎn yàn wǎng luò xì tǒng
工 作 人 员 在 **检 验** 网 络 系 统 。
Staff are **inspecting** the network system.

Noun
jiǎn yàn shí jiān dà gài shì liǎng gè bàn xiǎo shí
检 验 时 间 大 概 是 两 个 半 小 时 。
The **inspection** time is approximately two and a half hours.

376 减轻

jiǎn qīng

Verb: to lighten; to ease

^{wǒ}我 ^{xū}需 ^{yào}要 ^{zhù}助 ^{shǒu}手 ^{bāng}帮 ^{wǒ}我 ^{jiǎn}减 ^{qīng}轻 ^{gōng}工 ^{zuò}作 ^{fù}负 ^{dān}担。

I need an assistant to help me **lighten** my workload.

377 剪

jiǎn

Verb: to cut; to clip; to trim

^{zài}在 ^{xià}夏 ^{tiān}天， ^{wǒ}我 ^{cháng}常 ^{cháng}常 ^{gěi}给 ^{wǒ}我 ^{de}的 ^{gǒu}狗 ^{jiǎn}剪 ^{máo}毛。

In the summer, I often **clip** my dog's hair.

378 剪刀

jiǎn dāo

Noun: scissors; shears

^{wǒ}我 ^{de}的 ^{jiǎn}剪 ^{dāo}刀 ^{zài}在 ^{lán}蓝 ^{sè}色 ^{de}的 ^{gōng}工 ^{jù}具 ^{xiāng}箱 ^{lǐ}里。

My **scissors** are in the blue tool box.

379 剪子

jiǎn zi

Noun: scissors; shears

^{zhè}这 ^{bǎ}把 ^{jiǎn}剪 ^{zi}子 ^{tài}太 ^{zhòng}重， ^{wǒ}我 ^{ná}拿 ^{bu}不 ^{dòng}动。

This pair of **scissors** is too heavy for me to carry.

380 间接

jiàn jiē

Adjective: indirect

^{jiàn}间 ^{jiē}接 ^{de}的 ^{fāng}方 ^{fǎ}法 ^{bǐ}比 ^{zhí}直 ^{jiē}接 ^{de}的 ^{fāng}方 ^{fǎ}法 ^{yǒu}有 ^{xiào}效。

Indirect methods are more effective than direct methods.

381 建造

jiàn zào

Verb: to build; to construct

^{zhèng}政 ^{fǔ}府 ^{jì}计 ^{huà}划 ^{zài}在 ^{zhè}这 ^{lǐ}里 ^{jiàn}建 ^{zào}造 ^{xīn}新 ^{de}的 ^{jī}机 ^{chǎng}场。

The government plans **to build** a new airport here.

382 建筑　　jiàn zhù　　**Noun:** architecture

ōu shì jiàn zhù hé zhōng shì jiàn zhù dōu hěn měi
欧 式 **建 筑** 和 中 式 **建 筑** 都 很 美 。
Both European and Chinese-style **architecture** is beautiful.

383 健全　　jiàn quán　　**Adjective:** sound; well-established

tā suī rán zhì shāng gāo　dàn xīn zhì bú jiàn quán
他 虽 然 智 商 高 ， 但 心 智 不 **健 全** 。
Although he has a high IQ, he is not mentally **sound**.

384 键　　jiàn　　**Noun:** key (piano, keyboard)

wǒ de māo yòu zài gāng qín shàng àn jiàn le
我 的 猫 又 在 钢 琴 上 按 **键** 了 。
My cat is pressing keys on the **piano** again.

385 键盘　　jiàn pán　　**Noun:** keyboard

tā bāng wǒ ān zhuāng le xīn de diàn nǎo hé jiàn pán
他 帮 我 安 装 了 新 的 电 脑 和 **键 盘** 。
He helped me set up my new computer and **keyboard**.

386 将(要)　　jiāng (yào)　　**Verb:** will; would

wǒ men xià gè zhōu jiāng yào qù bā lí dù mì yuè le
我 们 下 个 周 **将 要** 去 巴 黎 度 蜜 月 了 。
We **will** go to Paris next week for honeymoon.

tā jiāng dài wǒ pá ài fēi ěr tǎ
他 **将** 带 我 爬 爱 菲 尔 塔 。
He **will** take me up the Eiffel Tower.

387 奖励　jiǎng lì

Verb: to reward
Noun: reward

Verb

lǎo bǎn jiǎng lì le tā men měi rén yì qiān yuán
老 板 **奖 励** 了 他 们 每 人 一 千 元 。
The boss **rewarded** each of them ￥1000.

Noun

duì yú tā men zhè yàng de jiǎng lì hěn fēng hòu
对 于 他 们 ， 这 样 的 **奖 励** 很 丰 厚 。
For them, this **reward** is very generous.

388 交代　jiāo dài

Verb: to brief;
to explain
(responsibility)

jǐng chá ràng qiǎng jié fàn jiāo dài zuò àn dòng jī
警 察 让 抢 劫 犯 **交 代** 作 案 动 机 。
The police asked the robber **to explain** the motive for the crime.

389 郊区　jiāo qū

Noun: suburb

wǒ de gōng yù zài jiāo qū tā de zài shì qū
我 的 公 寓 在 **郊 区** ， 他 的 在 市 区 。
My apartment is in the **suburbs**, his is in downtown.

390 胶带　jiāo dài

Noun: tape;
adhesive plaster

wǒ zài bāo zhuāng shèng dàn lǐ wù xū yào jiāo dài
我 在 包 装 圣 诞 礼 物 ， 需 要 **胶 带** 。
I'm wrapping Christmas presents and need **tape**.

391 胶水　jiāo shuǐ

Noun: glue

jiāo shuǐ bù hǎo yòng zǒng shì nòng zāng shǒu
胶 水 不 好 用 ， 总 是 弄 脏 手 。
The **glue** is not easy to use and always makes hands dirty.

392 脚步　jiǎo bù　**Noun:** footstep

wǒ de gǒu yì tīng dào jiǎo bù shēng jiù jiào
我 的 狗 一 听 到 **脚 步** 声 就 叫。
My dog barks as soon as he hears **footsteps**.

393 接触　jiē chù　**Verb:** to contact; get in contact with **Noun:** contact (experience)

Verb
tā gēn wǒ jiē chù de shí hòu yǒu diǎn jǐn zhāng
他 跟 我 **接 触** 的 时 候 有 点 紧 张。
He was a little nervous when he **came into contact** with me.

Noun
nà shì wǒ men dì yī cì miàn duì miàn jiē chù
那 是 我 们 第 一 次 面 对 面 **接 触**。
That was our first face-to-face **contact**.

394 接连　jiē lián　**Adverb:** one after another

zhè tiáo lù jiē lián fā shēng le jǐ cì chē huò
这 条 路 **接 连** 发 生 了 几 次 车 祸。
Several car accidents happen **one after another** on this road.

395 解除　jiě chú　**Verb:** to terminate; to remove

zǒng jīng lǐ zài kǎo lǜ yào bu yào jiě chú hé tong
总 经 理 在 考 虑 要 不 要 **解 除** 合 同。
The CEO is considering whether **to terminate** the contract.

396 解放　jiě fàng　**Verb:** to liberate; to emancipate

zěn yàng cái néng bāng tā men cóng pín kùn zhōng jiě fàng chū lái
怎 样 才 能 帮 他 们 从 贫 困 中 **解 放** 出 来？
How can we help them **liberate** themselves from poverty?

397 戒　　jiè　　**Verb:** to quit (bad habits)

tài hǎo le！ wǒ bà zhōng yú jué dìng jiè yān le
太 好 了 ！ 我 爸 终 于 决 定 **戒** 烟 了 。
Great! Dad finally decided **to quit** smoking.

398 届　　jiè　　**Classifier** for occasion/session (events)

nǐ huì kàn zhè yí jiè de chūn jié lián huān wǎn huì ma
你 会 看 这 一 **届** 的 春 节 联 欢 晚 会 吗 ？
Will you watch this **occasion of** the Spring Festival Gala?

399 今日　　jīn rì　　**Noun:** today (formal)

zhè shì jīn rì hé míng rì de jié mù dān
这 是 **今 日** 和 明 日 的 节 目 单 。
Here's the program list for **today** and tomorrow.

400 尽管　　jǐn guǎn　　**Conjunction:** despite; even though; although;

jǐn guǎn tā bìng le， tā hái shì jì xù shàng bān
尽 管 她 病 了 ， 她 还 是 继 续 上 班 。
Even though she's sick, she still continues to go to work.

401 紧紧　　jǐn jǐn　　**Adverb:** closely; tightly

wèi le ān wèi tā， wǒ jǐn jǐn de bào zhe tā
为 了 安 慰 她 ， 我 **紧 紧** 地 抱 着 她 。
To comfort her, I was holding her **tightly**.

402 尽可能　　jǐn kě néng　　**Adverb:** try one's best at something

wǒ yě chéng nuò huì jǐn kě néng bāng tā wán chéng rèn wù
我 也 承 诺 会 **尽 可 能** 帮 她 完 成 任 务 。
I also promised **to try my best** to help her complete the task.

403 进化   jìn huà   **Verb:** to evolve (species)
Noun: evolution

Verb
yǒu rén xiāng xìn rén lèi shì hóu zi **jìn huà** chéng de
有 人 相 信 人 类 是 猴 子 **进 化** 成 的 。
Some people believe that humans **evolved** from monkeys.

Noun
jìn huà lùn zhēn de kě xìn ma
进 化 论 真 的 可 信 吗 ？
Is the theory of **evolution** really credible?

404 近来   jìn lái   **Noun:** lately; recently

tā **jìn lái** tóu zī gǔ piào zhuàn le hěn duō qián
他 **近 来** 投 资 股 票 ， 赚 了 很 多 钱 。
Recently he invested in stocks and made a lot of money.

405 经费   jīng fèi   **Noun:** funds; costs

zhè xiē lì rùn shì tā kuò zhǎn yè wù de **jīng fèi**
这 些 利 润 是 他 扩 展 业 务 的 **经 费** 。
These profits are **funds** for his business expansion.

406 景象   jǐng xiàng   **Noun:** scene; sight

bú yào bèi biǎo miàn de hé xié **jǐng xiàng** mí huò
不 要 被 表 面 的 和 谐 **景 象** 迷 惑 。
Don't be fooled by the **sight** of a harmonious appearance.

407 警告   jǐng gào   **Verb:** to warn
Noun: warning

Verb
wǒ què shí **jǐng gào** guò qián fū bié wán huǒ
我 确 实 **警 告** 过 前 夫 别 玩 火 。
I did **warn** my ex-husband not to play with fire.

Noun
kě xī tā méi yǒu tīng wǒ de **jǐng gào**
可 惜 ， 他 没 有 听 我 的 **警 告** 。
Unfortunately, he didn't listen to my **warning**.

408 竞赛   jìng sài   **Noun:** match; contest; race

shéi shì zhè cì wǔ dǎo jìng sài de guàn jūn
谁 是 这 次 舞 蹈 **竞 赛** 的 冠 军 ？
Who is the champion of this dance **contest**?

409 竞争   jìng zhēng   **Verb:** to compete
Noun: competition

Verb
wǒ men huì hé wǔ gè jìng zhēng zhě jìng zhēng
我 们 会 和 五 个 竞 争 者 **竞 争** 。
We will **compete** with five competitors.

Noun
qǐng zhǔn bèi hǎo zhè cì jìng zhēng huì hěn jī liè
请 准 备 好 ， 这 次 **竞 争** 会 很 激 烈 。
Be well prepared, this **competition** will be fierce.

410 酒鬼   jiǔ guǐ   **Noun:** alcoholic; drunkard

wǒ tīng shuō tā de qián qī shì gè jiǔ guǐ
我 听 说 他 的 前 妻 是 个 **酒 鬼** 。
I heard his ex-wife was an **alcoholic**.

411 救灾   jiù zāi   **Verb:** to provide disaster relief

tā zǔ zhī rén yuán qù zāi qū jiù zāi le
他 组 织 人 员 去 灾 区 **救 灾** 了 。
He organized staff to the disaster area **to provide disaster relief**.

412 居然   jū rán   **Adverb:** actually (out of surprise)

tā men gōng sī jū rán juān le èr shí wàn ōu yuán
他 们 公 司 **居 然** 捐 了 二 十 万 欧 元 。
Their company **actually** donated 200,000 euros.

413 局面   jú miàn   **Noun:** situation (formal)

xiàn zài de zhèng zhì jú miàn hěn bù wěn dìng
现 在 的 政 治 **局 面** 很 不 稳 定 。
The current political **situation** is very unstable.

414 局长   jú zhǎng   **Noun:** director (of a bureau)

jú zhǎng gāng gāng yǐ jīng xuān bù cí zhí le
局 长 刚 刚 已 经 宣 布 辞 职 了 。
The **director** has just announced his resignation.

415 举动   jǔ dòng   **Noun:** move; behavior

tā de zhè gè jǔ dòng tài tū rán   wǒ bù dǒng
他 的 这 个 **举 动** 太 突 然 ， 我 不 懂 。
His **move** is so sudden that I don't understand it.

416 拒绝   jù jué   **Verb:** to refuse   **Noun:** refusal

Verb
wǒ de guī mì jù jué tóng shì de zhuī qiú
我 的 闺 蜜 **拒 绝** 同 事 的 追 求 。
My best friend **refuses** the pursuit of her colleague.

Noun
tā de jù jué ràng tā méi miàn zi
她 的 **拒 绝** 让 他 没 面 子 。
Her **refusal** made him lose face.

417 俱乐部   jù lè bù   **Noun:** club

wáng bīng shì jí tā jù lè bù de chuàng shǐ rén
王 兵 是 吉 他 **俱 乐 部** 的 创 始 人 。
Wang Bing is the founder of Guitar **Club**.

418 剧本

jù běn

Noun: script (of TV drama)

yǎn yuán men zài yǎn chū zhī qián yì bān huì kàn jù běn
演员们在演出之前一般会看**剧本**。

Actors usually read the **script** before performing.

419 决不

jué bù

Adverb: not at all; definitely not

yǒu de dǎo yǎn jué bù yǔn xǔ yǎn yuán gǎi tái cí
有的导演**决不**允许演员改台词。

Some directors do **not** allow actors to change their lines **at all**.

420 绝望

jué wàng

Adjective: desperate
Noun: desperation

Adj.

tā bú shì shī wàng ér shì jué wàng
他不是失望，而是**绝望**。

He is not disappointed, but **desperate**.

Noun

kàn bu dào xī wàng de gǎn jué jiù shì jué wàng
看不到希望的感觉就是**绝望**。

The feeling of not seeing hope is **desperation**.

421 军人

jūn rén

Noun: soldier; serviceman

wǒ wài gōng shì shì jiè èr zhàn de tuì wǔ jūn rén
我外公是世界二战的退伍**军人**。

My grandfather was a World War II veteran (retired **solider**).

422 开幕

kāi mù

Verb: to inaugurate; to begin (event)

wǒ xuān bù zhōng qiū wǎn huì zhèng shì kāi mù
我宣布中秋晚会正式**开幕**。

I declare the Mid-Autumn Festival Gala officially **begins**.

423 开幕式　kāi mù shì
Noun: opening ceremony

zhè cì kāi mù shì hěn chéng gōng, gǎn xiè dà jiā
这 次 **开 幕 式** 很 成 功 ， 感 谢 大 家 ！
This **opening ceremony** was successful, thank you everyone!

424 看成　kàn chéng
Verb: to regard as; to consider as

nǐ yào bǎ zhè cì shī bài kàn chéng yí gè jiào xùn
你 要 把 这 次 失 败 **看 成** 一 个 教 训 。
You should **regard** this failure **as** a lesson.

425 看出　kàn chū
Verb: to see (of discovery)

nǐ néng kàn chū tā zài àn liàn zhāng yún ma ？
你 能 **看 出** 他 在 暗 恋 张 云 吗 ？
Can you **see** that he has a hidden crush on Zhang Yun?

426 看待　kàn dài
Verb: to think of

wǒ bú zài hu bié rén zěn me kàn dài wǒ
我 不 在 乎 别 人 怎 么 **看 待** 我 。
I don't care what others **think of** me.

427 考核　kǎo hé
Verb: to examine; to assess (performance)

liú jīng lǐ fù zé kǎo hé yuán gōng de yè jì
刘 经 理 负 责 **考 核** 员 工 的 业 绩 。
Manager Liu's responsible for **assessing** employee performance.

428 烤肉　kǎo ròu
Noun: barbecued/ roast meat

shēng zhí hòu, tā qǐng wǒ men chī le kǎo ròu
升 职 后 ， 他 请 我 们 吃 了 **烤 肉** 。
After he was promoted, he treated us to **barbecued meat**.

429 烤鸭　kǎo yā　**Noun:** roasted duck

wǒ men diǎn le kǎo yā， kǎo yú hé kǎo tǔ dòu
我们点了**烤鸭**，烤鱼和烤土豆。
We ordered **roast duck**, roast fish and roast potatoes.

430 靠近　kào jìn　**Verb:** to be close to

cān guǎn kào jìn shì zhōng xīn， jiāo tōng hěn fāng biàn
餐馆**靠近**市中心，交通很方便。
The restaurant is **close to** the city center, with convenient transportation.

431 颗　kē　**Classifier** for very small objects

tā gěi wǒ de shēng rì lǐ wù shì yì kē zhēn zhū kòu zi
他给我的生日礼物是一**颗**珍珠扣子。
His birthday gift to me was a pearl button.

432 咳　ké　**Verb:** to cough

xiǎo yǔ zuì jìn dé le liú gǎn， tiān tiān ké
小雨最近得了流感，天天**咳**。
Xiaoyu recently has flu and is **coughing** every day.

433 可　kě　**Verb:** can/approve (use with other words)

tā de bìng jià yǐ jīng huò dé le zhǔ guǎn de xǔ kě
她的病假已经获得了主管的许**可**。
Her sick leave has been **approved** by her supervisor.

434 可怜　kě lián　**Adjective:** pitiful (deserving of sympathy)

tā de lǎo gōng hé ér zi dōu bèi chuán rǎn le， zhēn kě lián
她的老公和儿子都被传染了，真**可怜**！
Her husband and son were both infected, how **pitiful**!

435 可惜 kě xī

Adjective: regrettable; unfortunate
Adverb: regrettably; unfortunately

Adj.
zhè cì de zhì liáo fèi yòng tài gāo, zhēn kě xī
这 次 的 治 疗 费 用 太 高 ， 真 可 惜 ！
The cost of this treatment is too high, so **unfortunate**!

Adv.
kě xī zhè bú zài jiàn kāng bǎo xiǎn fàn wéi nèi
可 惜 这 不 在 健 康 保 险 范 围 内 。
Unfortunately this is not covered by health insurance.

436 渴望 kě wàng

Verb: to aspire for; to long for/to

wǔ nián lái, wǒ yì zhí kě wàng shí xiàn mèng xiǎng
五 年 来 ， 我 一 直 渴 望 实 现 梦 想 。
For five years, I have been **longing to** achieve my dream.

437 刻 kè

Verb: to carve; to engrave

wǒ zài zhè bǎ zhōng guó jiàn shàng kè le yí jù shī
我 在 这 把 中 国 剑 上 刻 了 一 句 诗 。
I **carved** a line of poetry on this Chinese sword.

438 客户 kè hù

Noun: client; customer

wǒ de kè hù shì gè shēn jià qiān wàn měi yuán de fù wēng
我 的 客 户 是 个 身 价 千 万 美 元 的 富 翁 。
My **client** is a rich man with a multi-million dollar net worth.

439 客气 kè qi

Adjective: polite; courteous

tā hěn gāo ào, shuō huà bú tài kè qi
他 很 高 傲 ， 说 话 不 太 客 气 。
He is arrogant and speaks rudely (not very **polite** manner).

440 客厅   kè tīng   **Noun:** living room

tā yǒu yí zuò bié shù   kè tīng fēi cháng háo huá
他 有 一 座 别 墅，客 厅 非 常 豪 华。
He has a villa with a very luxurious **living room**.

441 课题   kè tí   **Noun:** topic (academic)

nǐ yīng gāi xuǎn zé xué shēng gǎn xìng qù de kè tí
你 应 该 选 择 学 生 感 兴 趣 的 课 题。
You should choose **topics** that interest students.

442 肯定   kěn dìng   **Verb:** be sure; confirm
Adjective: definite

Verb
nǐ kěn dìng zhè jiàn shì hé nǐ méi guān xi ma
你 肯 定 这 件 事 和 你 没 关 系 吗？
Are you **sure** this matter has nothing to do with you?

Adj.
qǐng zài liǎng tiān nèi gěi wǒ yí gè kěn dìng de huí dá
请 在 两 天 内 给 我 一 个 肯 定 的 回 答。
Please give me a **definite** answer within 2 days.

443 空中   kōng zhōng   **Noun:** in the air; in the sky

wǒ kàn dào yí duì dà yàn zài kōng zhōng fēi lái fēi qù
我 看 到 一 对 大 雁 在 空 中 飞 来 飞 去。
I saw a pair of wild geese flying around **in the sky**.

444 控制   kòng zhì   **Verb:** to control
Noun: control

Verb
duì yú wǒ， kòng zhì gè rén gǎn qíng bù róng yì
对 于 我，控 制 个 人 感 情 不 容 易。
For me, it's not easy **to control** personal feelings.

Noun
hái zi xiǎng bǎi tuō fù mǔ de kòng zhì hěn zì rán
孩 子 想 摆 脱 父 母 的 控 制 很 自 然。
It's natural for children to want to escape parents' **control**.

445 口号　　kǒu hào　　**Noun:** slogan

tā de zǒng tǒng jìng xuǎn kǒu hào shì shén me
他 的 总 统 竞 选 **口 号** 是 什 么 ？
What's his presidential campaign **slogan**?

446 库　　kù　　**Noun:** warehouse; storeroom

chē kù lǐ yǒu yí gè bǎo ān shì
车 **库** 里 有 一 个 保 安 室 。
There is a security room in the car **warehouse**.

447 快活　　kuài huo　　**Adjective:** happy (enjoyment)

nǐ zuó wǎn zài yè diàn wán de kuài huo ma
你 昨 晚 在 夜 店 玩 得 **快 活** 吗 ？
Did you have a **happy** time at the nightclub last night?

448 宽度　　kuān dù　　**Noun:** width; breadth

wǒ zài cè liáng zhè zhāng zhuō zi de cháng dù hé kuān dù
我 在 测 量 这 张 桌 子 的 长 度 和 **宽 度** 。
I'm measuring the length and **width** of this table.

449 狂　　kuáng　　**Adjective:** arrogant; crazy; wild

tā mǎi cǎi piào yíng le yì bǎi wàn suǒ yǐ hěn kuáng
他 买 彩 票 赢 了 一 百 万 ， 所 以 很 **狂** ！
He won a million from lottery tickets, so he's gone **crazy**!

450 亏   kuī

Verb: to lose;
to have a deficit
Noun: loss; deficit
(use with other words)

Verb

dì yī cì chǎo gǔ, wǒ kuī le shí wàn yuán
第 一 次 炒 股， 我 **亏** 了 十 万 元。
The first time I traded in stocks, I **lost** ¥100,000.

Noun

zhè cì kuī běn ràng wǒ yù mèn le yí gè zhōu
这 次 **亏 本** 让 我 郁 闷 了 一 个 周。
This **loss** made me depressed for a week.

451 困扰   kùn rǎo

Verb: to bother;
to perplex; to puzzle

bié ràng zhè yàng de dào méi shì kùn rǎo nǐ
别 让 这 样 的 倒 霉 事 **困 扰** 你。
Don't let this bad-luck matter **bother** you.

452a 落   là

Verb: to be missing;
to leave behind

zāo gāo ! wǒ bǎ shǒu jī là zài chē lǐ le
糟 糕 ！ 我 把 手 机 **落** 在 车 里 了。
Oops! I **left behind** my phone in the car.

452b 落   luò

Verb: to fall (off)

fēng shù shàng de yè zi chà bu duō dōu luò le
枫 树 上 的 叶 子 差 不 多 都 **落** 了。
Almost all the leaves on the maple trees have **fallen off**.

453 来信   lái xìn

Verb: to send a letter here
Noun: incoming letter

Verb

tā lái xìn le, qǐng wǒ men hē xǐ jiǔ
他 **来 信** 了，请 我 们 喝 喜 酒。
He **sent a letter here**, inviting us to his wedding banquet.

Noun

tā de lái xìn ràng wǒ hěn kāi xīn
他 的 **来 信** 让 我 很 开 心。
His **incoming letter** makes me very happy.

454 烂   làn

Adjective: bad; rotten

zhè gè pī sà bǐng yǐ jīng làn le, rēng le ba
这 个 披 萨 饼 已 经 **烂** 了，扔 了 吧。
This pizza is already **rotten**, throw it away.

455 朗读   lǎng dú

Verb: to read aloud

měi tiān lǎng dú wén zhāng kě yǐ tí gāo zhōng wén kǒu yǔ
每 天 **朗 读** 文 章 可 以 提 高 中 文 口 语。
Reading articles **aloud** daily can improve your spoken Chinese.

456 浪漫   làng màn

Adjective: romantic

tā yǐ qián hěn làng màn, xiàn zài què hěn kū zào
他 以 前 很 **浪 漫**，现 在 却 很 枯 燥。
He used to be **romantic**, but now he is boring.

457 劳动   láo dòng

Verb: to do physical labor
Noun: labor

Verb

wǒ cóng lái dōu bù xǐ huān zài tián lǐ láo dòng
我 从 来 都 不 喜 欢 在 田 里 **劳 动**。
I've never liked **doing physical labor** in the fields.

Noun

wǔ yuè yī hào shì guó jì láo dòng jié
五 月 一 号 是 国 际 **劳 动** 节。
May 1st is International **Labor** Day.

458 梨　　　　　lí　　　　　**Noun:** pear

wǒ ér zi zài gěi nǎi nai xuē lí hé bō luó
我 儿 子 在 给 奶 奶 削 **梨** 和 菠 萝 。
My son is peeling **pears** and pineapples for his grandma.

459 礼　　　　　lǐ　　　　　**Noun:** ceremony; rite; gift (use with other words)

qǐng kè hé sòng lǐ shì wéi chí guān xi de shǒu duàn
请 客 和 送 **礼** 是 维 持 关 系 的 手 段 。
Treats and **gift**-giving are ways to maintain relationships.

460 礼拜　　　　　lǐ bài　　　　　**Noun:** week; religious service

jiào huáng xià gè lǐ bài huì qù bā lí shèng mǔ yuàn
教 皇 下 个 **礼 拜** 会 去 巴 黎 圣 母 院 。
The Pope will go to Notre Dame next **week**.

461 礼貌　　　　　lǐ mào　　　　　**Adjective:** polite

tā yòu qiān xū yòu lǐ mào fēi cháng shòu huān yíng
他 又 谦 虚 又 **礼 貌** ， 非 常 受 欢 迎 。
He is humble and **polite**, so very popular.

462 厉害　　　　　lì hai　　　　　**Adjective:** great; awesome; fierce

lǐ jūn xiǎng chéng wéi lì hai de wǔ shù gāo shǒu
李 君 想 成 为 **厉 害** 的 武 术 高 手 。
Li Jun wants to become a **great** martial arts master.

463 立　　　　　lì　　　　　**Verb:** to stand; to erect

tā yí gè rén zài qiáng xià liàn xí dào lì
他 一 个 人 在 墙 下 练 习 倒 **立** 。
He is practicing hand**standing** alone under the wall.

464 立场

lì chǎng

Noun: stance; position

wáng shì chéng yuán hěn shǎo gōng kāi tā men de zhèng zhì lì chǎng
王室成员很少公开他们的政治**立场**。

Members of the royal family rarely make their political **stance** public.

465 利润

lì rùn

Noun: profit

gōng sī jīn nián de lì rùn bǐ qù nián shàng zhǎng le bèi
公司今年的**利润**比去年上涨了3倍。

The company's **profits** this year have tripled compared to last year.

466 例外

lì wài

Noun: exception

měi gè rén dōu huì màn màn lǎo qù méi yǒu lì wài
每个人都会慢慢老去，没有**例外**。

Everyone will age slowly, there is no **exception**.

467 连接

lián jiē

Verb: to link; to join; to connect
Noun: attachment; connection

Verb

wǒ xū yào lián jiē wǎng luò mì mǎ shì shén me
我需要**连接**网络，密码是什么？

I need to **connect** to the Internet, what is the password?

Noun

bào fēng yǔ gān rǎo le xìn hào lián jiē
暴风雨干扰了信号**连接**。

The storm disrupted the signal **connection**.

468 联络

lián luò

Verb: to get in contact with
Noun: contact; liaison

Verb

^{wǒ} ^{yǐ} ^{jīng} ^{hěn} ^{jiǔ} ^{méi} ^{yǒu} ^{lián} ^{luò} ^{qián} ^{nǚ} ^{yǒu} ^{le}
我 已 经 很 久 没 有 **联 络** 前 女 友 了。
I haven't **contacted** my ex-girlfriend for a long time.

Noun

^{wǒ} ^{zǎo} ^{jiù} ^{shān} ^{chú} ^{le} ^{tā} ^{de} ^{lián} ^{luò} ^{fāng} ^{shì}
我 早 就 删 除 了 她 的 **联 络** 方 式。
I have long deleted her **contact** information.

469 联想

lián xiǎng

Verb: to associate (ideas, images, concepts)
Noun: association

Verb

^{zhè} ^{fú} ^{huà} ^{ràng} ^{wǒ} ^{lián} ^{xiǎng} ^{dào} ^{le} ^{yì} ^{shǒu} ^{táng} ^{shī}
这 幅 画 让 我 **联 想** 到 了 一 首 唐 诗。
For me, this painting is **associated** with a Tang poem.

Noun

^{nǐ} ^{de} ^{lián} ^{xiǎng} ^{guǒ} ^{rán} ^{fēi} ^{cháng} ^{shēng} ^{dòng}
你 的 **联 想** 果 然 非 常 生 动！
Your **associations** are indeed very vivid!

470 脸盆

liǎn pén

Noun: washbasin

^{hěn} ^{duō} ^{lǎo} ^{rén} ^{réng} ^{rán} ^{xí} ^{guàn} ^{yòng} ^{liǎn} ^{pén}
很 多 老 人 仍 然 习 惯 用 **脸 盆**。
Many old people are still accustomed to using **washbasins**.

471 脸色

liǎn sè

Noun: look; facial expression

^{rú} ^{guǒ} ^{tā} ^{liǎn} ^{sè} ^{yīn} ^{àn} ^{jiù} ^{biǎo} ^{míng} ^{tā} ^{shēng} ^{qì}
如 果 他 **脸 色** 阴 暗， 就 表 明 他 生 气。
If his **facial expression** appears gloomy, it means he is angry.

472 恋爱

liàn ài

Verb: be in a relationship (romantic)

^{liàn} ^{ài} ^{sān} ^{nián} ^{hòu} ^{wǒ} ^{men} ^{dìng} ^{hūn} ^{le}
恋 爱 三 年 后， 我 们 订 婚 了。
After **being in a relationship** for 3 years, we got engaged.

473 两岸   liǎng àn   **Noun:** both sides; both coasts

liǎng àn de qīn péng hǎo yǒu dōu cān jiā le wǒ men de hūn lǐ
两岸的亲朋好友都参加了我们的婚礼。
Family and friends from **both coasts** attended our wedding.

474 邻居   lín jū   **Noun:** neighbor

wǒ gēn lín jū hěn shú bù guò guān xi yì bān
我跟**邻居**很熟，不过关系一般。
I'm familiar with my **neighbor**, but our relationship is average.

475 铃   líng   **Noun:** bell

gāng gāng yǒu rén àn le mén líng qù kàn kan
刚刚有人按了门**铃**，去看看。
Someone just rang the door**bell**, go take a look.

476 铃声   líng shēng   **Noun:** ringtone; the tinkle of bells

nǐ de shǒu jī líng shēng zhēn hǎo tīng shì shén me gē
你的手机**铃声**真好听，是什么歌？
Your cell phone **ringtone** is really nice, what song is it?

477 领带   lǐng dài   **Noun:** necktie; tie

wǒ dǎ suàn sòng tā yì tiáo jīng zhì de lǐng dài
我打算送他一条精致的**领带**。
I'm going to gift him an exquisite **tie**.

478 令   lìng   **Verb:** to cause; to order; to command

jiāng jūn lìng shì bīng cóng biān jìng chè tuì
将军**令**士兵从边境撤退。
The general **ordered** the soldiers to retreat from the border.

479 流动   liú dòng   **Verb:** to flow (water)

wǒ xǐ huān yì biān dǎ zuò yì biān tīng shuǐ liú dòng
我 喜 欢 一 边 打 坐， 一 边 听 水 **流 动** 。
I like to meditate while listening to the water **flowing**.

480 流通   liú tōng   **Verb:** to circulate (air, money, commodities)

qǐng kāi chuāng ràng kōng qì liú tōng
请 开 窗， 让 空 气 **流 通** 。
Please open windows to allow air to **circulate**.

481 漏   lòu   **Verb:** to leak; to drip

shén me ？ nǐ de xīn fáng zi jū rán lòu yǔ ？
什 么 ？ 你 的 新 房 子 居 然 **漏** 雨 ？
What? Your new house is actually **leaking** (rain)?

482 漏洞   lòu dòng   **Noun:** leak; flaw; loophole

jīng míng de lǜ shī zhī dào zěn me zuān fǎ lǜ lòu dòng
精 明 的 律 师 知 道 怎 么 钻 法 律 **漏 洞** 。
Savvy lawyers know how to exploit legal **loopholes**.

483 逻辑   luó ji   **Noun:** logic

xué shù xué kě yǐ péi yǎng luó ji sī wéi
学 数 学 可 以 培 养 **逻 辑** 思 维 。
Learning mathematics can develop **logical** thinking.

484 落实   luò shí   **Verb:** to implement; to put into effect

xīn de yí mín zhèng cè huì zài míng nián luò shí
新 的 移 民 政 策 会 在 明 年 **落 实** 。
The new immigration policy will be **implemented** next year.

485 码头　　mǎ tóu　　**Noun:** wharf; pier

mǎ tóu shàng tíng kào zhe jǐ shí tiáo chuán
码 头 上 停 靠 着 几 十 条 船 。
There are dozens of boats docked at the **pier**.

486 骂　　mà　　**Verb:** to scold

tā zài gōng gòng chǎng suǒ mà tā lǎo pó shì mǔ lǎo hǔ
他 在 公 共 场 所 骂 他 老 婆 是 母 老 虎 。
He **scolded** his wife as a tigress in a public place.

487 买卖　　mǎi mài　　**Noun:** buy and sell; business; transaction

zhè gè shēng yì rén cóng shì jiā jù de mǎi mài
这 个 生 意 人 从 事 家 具 的 买 卖 。
This businessman is engaged in **buying and selling** furniture.

488 漫长　　màn cháng　　**Adjective:** very long; endless

zhuàn mǎn shí yì měi yuán shì tiáo màn cháng de lù
赚 满 十 亿 美 元 是 条 漫 长 的 路 。
Making a full billion dollars is a **very long** journey.

489 漫画　　màn huà　　**Noun:** comic; cartoon

wǒ gěi shuāng bāo tāi nǚ ér mǎi le hěn duō màn huà shū
我 给 双 胞 胎 女 儿 买 了 很 多 漫 画 书 。
I bought a lot of **comic** books for my twin girls.

490 毛笔　　máo bǐ　　**Noun:** Chinese calligraphy brush

tā men liù suì jiù kāi shǐ xué yòng máo bǐ huà huà
她 们 六 岁 就 开 始 学 用 毛 笔 画 画 。
They started learning to draw with Chinese calligraphy **brushes** at the age of six.

491 矛盾   máo dùn   **Verb:** to contradict
Noun: conflict; contradiction

Verb

^{bù} 部 ^{zhǎng} 长 ^{de} 的 ^{huà} 话 ^{hé} 和 ^{tā} 他 ^{de} 的 ^{xíng} 行 ^{wéi} 为 ^{xiāng} 相 ^{hù} 互 **矛盾** 。

部长的话和他的行为相互**矛盾**。
The minister's words and actions **contradict** each other.

Noun

我们虽然有**矛盾**，却仍然是朋友。
wǒ men suī rán yǒu máo dùn，què réng rán shì péng yǒu

Although we have **conflicts**, we are still friends.

492 冒   mào   **Verb:** to give off; to take risk (use with other words)

tā mào xiǎn cóng dǎi tú de shǒu lǐ duó guò dāo
他冒险从歹徒的手里夺过刀。
He **took the risk** by snatching the knife from the criminal's hand.

493 贸易   mào yì   **Noun:** trade; commerce

wǒ men yào jiàn lì píng děng hù lì de mào yì guān xi
我们要建立平等互利的**贸易**关系。
We need to establish an equal and mutually beneficial **trade** relationship.

494 煤   méi   **Noun:** coal

zài shān shàng wā méi de gōng rén dōu shòu shāng le
在山上挖**煤**的工人都受伤了。
The workers digging **coal** in the mountain were all injured.

495 煤气   méi qì   **Noun:** coal gas

tīng shuō zhè shì méi qì zhòng dú dǎo zhì de
听说这是**煤气**中毒导致的。
I heard it was caused by **coal gas** poisoning.

496 门诊

mén zhěn

Noun: outpatient service

qǐng wèn shéi shì mén zhěn bù mén de fù zé rén
请问谁是门诊部门的负责人？
Who is the person in charge of the **outpatient** department?

497 迷人

mí rén

Adjective: charming

suàn mìng xiān shēng shuō wǒ jiāng lái de lǎo gōng yòu mí rén
算命先生说我将来的老公又迷人
yòu yǒu qián
又有钱。
The fortune teller said my future husband is **charming** and rich.

498 迷信

mí xìn

Noun: superstition

tā de huà shì mí xìn wán quán bù kě kào
他的话是迷信，完全不可靠。
His words are **superstition**, completely unreliable.

499 面貌

miàn mào

Noun: appearance (of face)

píng jià rén de shí hòu bú yào zhǐ kàn miàn mào
评价人的时候，不要只看面貌。
When evaluating people, don't just look at their **appearance**.

500 面子

miàn zi

Noun: face (prestige, self-esteem, dignity)

tā bù chéng rèn cuò wù shì pà diū miàn zi
他不承认错误是怕丢面子！
He won't admit his mistake because he's afraid of losing **face**!

501 秒

miǎo

Noun: second (of time)

xiǎng ràng tā zài shí miǎo nèi dào qiàn shì bù kě néng de
想 让 他 在 十 秒 内 道 歉 是 不 可 能 的 。
It's impossible to get him to apologize within 10 **seconds**.

502 敏感

mǐn gǎn

Adjective: sensitive

zhè zhǒng rén zì zūn xīn qiáng tài mǐn gǎn le
这 种 人 自 尊 心 强 , 太 敏 感 了 !
This kind of man has strong self-esteem and is too **sensitive**!

503 明亮

míng liàng

Adjective: bright; vivid

gōng yù de kè tīng míng liàng dàn shū fáng hūn àn
公 寓 的 客 厅 明 亮 , 但 书 房 昏 暗 。
The apartment's living room is **bright**, but the study is dark.

504 明明

míng míng

Adverb: obviously; clearly

tā míng míng zhī dào zhēn xiàng què jiǎ zhuāng bù míng bái
他 明 明 知 道 真 相 , 却 假 装 不 明 白 。
He **clearly** knows the truth, but pretends not to understand.

505 命令

mìng lìng

Verb: to order; to command
Noun: order; command

Verb

zǒng jīng lǐ mìng lìng wǒ men lì kè jiě chú hé yuē
总 经 理 命 令 我 们 立 刻 解 除 合 约 。
The CEO **ordered** us to terminate the contract immediately.

Noun

xià shǔ bì xū fú cóng shàng sī de mìng lìng ma
下 属 必 须 服 从 上 司 的 命 令 吗 ?
Do subordinates have to follow **orders** from their superiors?

506 模范　mó fàn

Noun: role model (of good example)

tā hěn qín láo, shì wǒ men gōng sī de mó fàn
他 很 勤 劳， 是 我 们 公 司 的 模 范。
He is diligent, a **role model** for our company.

507 模仿　mó fǎng

Verb: to imitate; to copy

wǒ fā xiàn yǒu shāng jiā zài mó fǎng wǒ men de chǎn pǐn
我 发 现 有 商 家 在 模 仿 我 们 的 产 品。
I found that some merchants are **imitating** our products.

508 模糊　mó hu

Verb: to blur
Adjective: vague; blurry

Verb
yǎn lèi mó hu le wǒ de yǎn jīng
眼 泪 模 糊 了 我 的 眼 睛。
Tears **blurred** my eyes.

Adj.
wǒ dāng shí kàn bù qīng nà gè mó hu de rén yǐng
我 当 时 看 不 清 那 个 模 糊 的 人 影。
I couldn't see the **blurry** figure clearly at that time.

509 模式　mó shì

Noun: model; mode (pattern or structure)

zhè shì sān shí nián lái de gǔ shì jīng jì mó shì
这 是 三 十 年 来 的 股 市 经 济 模 式。
This is the economic **model** of the stock market for 30 years.

510 摩擦　mó cā

Noun: clash; scratch

tóng shì zhī jiān fā shēng xiǎo mó cā hěn zhèng cháng
同 事 之 间 发 生 小 摩 擦 很 正 常。
It's normal to have minor **clashes** between colleagues.

511 摩托   mó tuō   **Noun:** motorbike

什么？你表弟把**摩托**开进了河里？
shén me? nǐ biǎo dì bǎ mó tuō kāi jìn le hé lǐ
What? Your cousin drove his **motorbike** into the river?

512 模样   mú yàng   **Noun:** appearance

我能想象他受伤的**模样**，真可怜。
wǒ néng xiǎng xiàng tā shòu shāng de mú yàng, zhēn kě lián
I can imagine his injured **appearance**, so pitiful.

513 目光   mù guāng   **Noun:** expression (eyes)

他的**目光**又尴尬又难过。
tā de mù guāng yòu gān gà yòu nán guò
His **expression** looked embarrassed and sad.

514 耐心   nài xīn   **Adjective:** patient   **Noun:** patience

Adj. 他在培训的时候不够**耐心**。
tā zài péi xùn de shí hòu bú gòu nài xīn
He was not **patient** enough during training.

Noun 缺乏**耐心**一直是他的缺点。
quē fá nài xīn yì zhí shì tā de quē diǎn
Lacking **patience** has always been his shortcoming.

515 男性   nán xìng   **Noun:** man; male

我们机构的**男性**是女性的两倍。
wǒ men jī gòu de nán xìng shì nǚ xìng de liǎng bèi
There are twice as many **men** as women in our institution.

516 南北   nán běi   **Noun:** south and north

nán běi de qì hòu yǒu hěn dà de qū bié
南北的气候有很大的区别。
There are big differences in climate between **the south and north**.

517 南极   nán jí   **Noun:** Antarctica; South Pole

wǒ men tuán duì xiǎng qù nán jí kàn qǐ é
我们团队想去**南极**看企鹅。
Our team wants to go to see penguins in **Antarctica**.

518 难得   nán dé   **Adjective:** rare (hard to come by)

tā men duì xiàng mù de fù chū hěn nán dé
他们对项目的付出很**难得**。
Their dedication to the project is **rare**.

519 难以   nán yǐ   **Adverb:** hard to; difficult to

wǒ nán yǐ xiǎng xiàng zài zhè zhǒng huán jìng xià shēng cún
我**难以**想象在这种环境下生存。
I find it **hard to** imagine surviving in this environment.

520 脑子   nǎo zi   **Noun:** brain

tā mà nǐ shì hún dàn nǎo zi jìn shuǐ le ba
他骂你是混蛋？**脑子**进水了吧！
He scolded you as a bastard? He's insane (**brain** flooded)!

521 内在   nèi zài   **Adjective:** inner; internal

tā de nèi zài měi bǐ wài zài měi gèng zhēn guì
她的**内在**美比外在美更珍贵。
Her **inner** beauty is more precious than her outer beauty.

522 能量   néng liàng   **Noun:** energy

tā xǐ huān zài shè jiāo méi tǐ shàng chuán dì zhèng néng liàng
她 喜 欢 在 社 交 媒 体 上 传 递 正 **能 量** 。
She likes spreading positive **energy** on social media.

523 年度   nián dù   **Noun:** year; annual

zǒng jiān ràng wǒ xiě nián dù zǒng jié bào gào
总 监 让 我 写 **年 度** 总 结 报 告 。
The director asked me to write the **annual** summary report.

524 年龄   nián líng   **Noun:** age

wǒ men de nián líng xiāng tóng dōu shì èr shí wǔ suì
我 们 的 **年 龄** 相 同 ， 都 是 二 十 五 岁 。
We are the same **age**, both 25.

525 年前   nián qián   **Noun:** years ago; before the New Year

tā dǎ suàn zài nián qián cí zhí
他 打 算 在 **年 前** 辞 职 。
He plans to resign **before the New Year**.

526 牛   niú   **Adjective:** great; awesome; brave
Noun: cow; ox

Adj.
tā yǐ jīng zhǎo dào xīn gōng zuò le zhēn niú
他 已 经 找 到 新 工 作 了 ？ 真 **牛** ！
He already found a new job? Really **awesome**!

Noun
tā shǔ niú yǒu diǎn gù zhí
他 属 **牛** ， 有 点 固 执 。
He's born in the year of **ox** and a bit stubborn.

527 牛仔裤   niú zǎi kù   **Noun:** jeans

zhè shì xīn kuǎn niú zǎi kù hěn shí máo
这 是 新 款 **牛 仔 裤** ， 很 时 髦 。
These are new-style **jeans**, very fashionable.

528 农产品   nóng chǎn pǐn   **Noun:** farm produce; agricultural products

zhè xiē fēi zhōu de nóng chǎn pǐn zhì liàng hěn hǎo
这 些 非 洲 的 **农 产 品** 质 量 很 好 。
The quality of these African **agricultural products** is good.

529 女性   nǚ xìng   **Noun:** woman; female

hěn duō shēng wán hái zi de nǚ xìng yǒu chǎn hòu yì yù zhèng
很 多 生 完 孩 子 的 **女 性** 有 产 后 抑 郁 症 。
Many **women** who gave birth suffer from postpartum depression.

530 暖   nuǎn   **Adjective:** warm

yīn wèi shēn tǐ xū tā xū yào bǎo nuǎn
因 为 身 体 虚 ， 她 需 要 保 **暖** 。
Because her body is weak, she needs to keep **warm**.

531 偶尔   ǒu ěr   **Adverb:** occasionally; from time to time

wǒ men ǒu ěr kāi shì pín liáo tiān
我 们 **偶 尔** 开 视 频 聊 天 。
We **occasionally** have video chats.

532 偶然   ǒu rán   **Adjective:** accidental; by chance

wǒ zhī dào tā lǎo gōng chū guǐ bù shì ǒu rán
我 知 道 她 老 公 出 轨 不 是 **偶 然** 。
I know her husband's cheating was not **by chance**.

533 偶像
ǒu xiàng   **Noun:** idol

wǒ gè rén jué de chóng bài ǒu xiàng shì bú jiàn kāng de
我 个 人 觉 得 崇 拜 **偶 像** 是 不 健 康 的 。
I personally feel that **idol** worship is unhealthy.

534 拍摄
pāi shè   **Verb:** to film; to shoot (a film)

tīng shuō tā men jù zǔ zài zhī jiā gē pāi shè diàn yǐng
听 说 他 们 剧 组 在 芝 加 哥 **拍 摄** 电 影 。
I heard that their crew is **filming** a movie in Chicago.

535 排除
pái chú   **Verb:** to remove; to eliminate

ān zhuāng dì xià tōng dào shì wèi le pái chú fèi shuǐ
安 装 地 下 通 道 是 为 了 **排 除** 废 水 。
Underground passages are installed **to remove** waste water.

536 旁
páng   **Noun:** side; other; else (use with other words)

zuò hǎo zì jǐ bú yào guǎn páng rén de píng lùn
做 好 自 己 , 不 要 管 **旁 人** 的 评 论 。
Just be yourself and ignore the comments of **others**.

537 陪
péi   **Verb:** to accompany

tā ràng wǒ péi tā qù cān jiā xiāng qīn jié mù
他 让 我 **陪** 他 去 参 加 相 亲 节 目 。
He asked me **to accompany** him to attend a dating show.

538 赔
péi   **Verb:** to pay (for loss)

sù sòng shī bài hòu tā péi le qián qī wǔ wàn yuán
诉 讼 失 败 后 , 他 **赔** 了 前 妻 五 万 元 。
After the lawsuit failed, he **paid** his ex-wife ¥50,000.

539 赔偿　péi cháng

Verb: to compensate
Noun: compensation

Verb

tā bì xū péi cháng duì fāng de jīng jì sǔn shī
他必须**赔偿**对方的经济损失。
He must **compensate** the other party for economic losses.

Noun

wǒ jué de zhè cì péi cháng bǐ jiào gōng píng
我觉得这次**赔偿**比较公平。
I think this **compensation** is relatively fair.

540 配备　pèi bèi

Verb: to equip
Noun: equipment

Verb

tā men huì lái xué xiào pèi bèi wǎng luò xì tǒng
他们会来学校**配备**网络系统。
They will come to the school **to equip** the network system.

Noun

wǒ duì tā men de pèi bèi yǒu xìn xīn
我对他们的**配备**有信心。
I have confidence in their **equipment**.

541 配套　pèi tào

Verb: to provide a set (equipment)
Noun: equipment set

Verb

tā men de gōng zuò zhǔ yào shì pèi tào yìng jiàn
他们的工作主要是**配套**硬件。
Their job mainly involves hardware integration (**providing set of hardware**).

Noun

jiǔ diàn de fú wù pèi tào hěn wán shàn
酒店的服务**配套**很完善。
The hotel's service **equipment set** is comprehensive.

542 喷　pēn

Verb: to spray; to sprinkle

nǐ kàn guò dà xiàng pēn shuǐ ma
你看过大象**喷**水吗？
Have you ever seen an elephant **spray** water?

543 盆　　　pén　　　**Noun:** basin; tub

wǒ de yù shì yǒu yí gè bái sè de dà zǎo pén
我 的 浴 室 有 一 个 白 色 的 大 澡 **盆** 。
My bathroom has a large white (bath) **tub**.

544 披　　　pī　　　**Verb:** to wrap around

tā chōu zhe yān　pī zhe dà yī zǒu zài lù shàng
他 抽 着 烟 ， **披** 着 大 衣 走 在 路 上 。
He's smoking and **wrapped in** his coat walking on the road

545 皮肤　　　pí fū　　　**Noun:** skin

tā de pí fū cū cāo　liǎn shàng yǒu yí dào bā
他 的 **皮 肤** 粗 糙 ， 脸 上 有 一 道 疤 。
His **skin** was rough and there was a scar on his face.

546 皮鞋　　　pí xié　　　**Noun:** leather shoes

ér qiě tā chuān de pí xié yòu zāng yòu pò
而 且 他 穿 的 **皮 鞋** 又 脏 又 破 。
And the **leather shoes** he wore were dirty and torn.

547 脾气　　　pí qi　　　**Noun:** temper

tā pí qi huài　róng yì duì rén fā huǒ
他 **脾 气** 坏 ， 容 易 对 人 发 火 。
He has a bad **temper** and gets angry at others easily.

548 匹　　　pǐ　　　**Classifier** for horses

zhè pǐ bái mǎ de jià gé shì bā qiān ōu yuán
这 **匹** 白 马 的 价 格 是 八 千 欧 元 。
The price of the white horse is 8,000 euros.

549 骗   piàn   **Verb:** to lie; to fool

hái zi hěn shǎo piàn rén， tā men hěn dān chún
孩子很少骗人，他们很单纯。
Children rarely **lie**, they are very innocent.

550 骗子   piàn zi   **Noun:** liar; scammer; cheater

xiāng fǎn， duō shù piàn zi dōu shì chéng rén
相反，多数骗子都是成人。
On the contrary, most **scammers** are adults.

551 拼   pīn   **Verb:** to work hard (use with other words)

wǒ men yào pīn lì wán chéng zhè cì jǐn jí rèn wù
我们要拼力完成这次紧急任务。
We need **to work hard** to complete this urgent mission.

552 频道   pín dào   **Noun:** channel

yǒu yí yì rén dìng yuè le tā de pín dào
有一亿人订阅了他的频道。
100 million people have subscribed to his **channel**.

553 频繁   pín fán   **Adjective:** frequent   **Adverb:** frequently

Adj.
zuì jìn de zhèng zhì chǒu wén hěn pín fán
最近的政治丑闻很频繁。
Political scandals are very **frequent** recently.

Adv.
qián zǒng tǒng bèi pín fán gào shàng fǎ tíng
前总统被频繁告上法庭。
The ex-president is **frequently** sued to court.

554 品   pǐn

Verb: to taste; to try
Noun: category;
product
(use with other words)

Verb

wǒ men yì biān chī yuè bǐng, yì biān pǐn xīn chá
我 们 一 边 吃 月 饼 ， 一 边 **品** 新 茶 。
We were eating mooncakes whilst **tasting** new tea.

Noun

zhè xiē chéng pǐn shì zhì liàng zuì hǎo de
这 些 **成 品** 是 质 量 最 好 的 。
These **finished products** are of the best quality.

555 品种   pǐn zhǒng

Noun: breed;
species; category

nǐ zuì xǐ huān shén me pǐn zhǒng de gǒu
你 最 喜 欢 什 么 **品 种** 的 狗 ？
What's your favorite **breed** of dog?

556 平坦   píng tǎn

Adjective: flat;
smooth (surface)

zhè tiáo gōng lù shì xīn jiàn de, dāng rán píng tǎn
这 条 公 路 是 新 建 的 ， 当 然 **平 坦** 。
This road is new and of course feels **smooth**.

557 平原   píng yuán

Noun:
plain or plateau (land)

kāi fā yǐ qián, zhè lǐ céng shì yí piàn píng yuán
开 发 以 前 ， 这 里 曾 是 一 片 **平 原** 。
Before development, this area was a **plain**.

558 评估   píng gū

Verb: to evaluate
Noun: evaluation

Verb

píng wěi men zài píng gū cān sài zhě de biǎo yǎn
评 委 们 在 **评 估** 参 赛 者 的 表 演 。
The judges are **evaluating** the contestants' performances.

Noun

tā men de píng gū huì zài shí fēn zhōng hòu gōng kāi
他 们 的 **评 估** 会 在 十 分 钟 后 公 开 。
Their **evaluation** will be made public in 10 minutes.

559 评论   píng lùn   **Verb:** to comment
Noun: comment

Verb
tīng shuō zhǔ xí jù jué píng lùn zhè jiàn shì
听 说 主 席 拒 绝 **评 论** 这 件 事 。
The chairman is said to have declined **to comment** on the matter.

Noun
mù qián suǒ yǒu de píng lùn dōu bèi shān chú le
目 前 所 有 的 **评 论** 都 被 删 除 了 。
All **comments** have been deleted so far.

560 凭   píng   **Preposition:** by; via; based on

tā píng shén me fǎn duì zì yóu yán lùn
她 **凭** 什 么 反 对 自 由 言 论 ？
What does she **base** her opposition to freedom of speech **on**?

561 泼   pō   **Verb:** to splash

tā yì chū mén jiù bèi kàng yì zhě pō shuǐ le
她 一 出 门 ， 就 被 抗 议 者 **泼** 水 了 。
As soon as she went out, she was **splashed** with water by protesters.

562 葡萄   pú tao   **Noun:** grape

wǒ ài chī xiāng jiāo pú tao yīng táo hé lí
我 爱 吃 香 蕉 ， **葡 萄** ， 樱 桃 和 梨 。
I love eating bananas, **grapes**, cherries and pears.

563 葡萄酒   pú tao jiǔ   **Noun:** grape wine

pú tao jiǔ de zhì zào chéng xù fù zá ma
葡 萄 酒 的 制 造 程 序 复 杂 吗 ？
Is the process of making **grape wine** complex?

564 期望   qī wàng   **Verb:** to expect; to hope
Noun: expectation

Verb
dà jiā dōu qī wàng kàn jiàn jīng jì fù sū
大家都**期望**看见经济复苏。
Everyone **expects** to see economic recovery.

Noun
wǒ méi yǒu gū fù fù mǔ duì wǒ de qī wàng
我没有辜负父母对我的**期望**。
I didn't fail my parents' **expectations** of me.

565 齐全   qí quán   **Adjective:** complete; all ready

děng wén jiàn qí quán hòu wǒ jiù bàn qiān zhèng
等文件**齐全**后，我就办签证。
Once the documents are **complete**, I will apply for the visa.

566 其   qí   **Pronoun:** his; her; its etc. (formal)

tā shì wén xué tiān cái qí fù yě shì jiào yù jiā
他是文学天才，**其**父也是教育家。
He is a literary genius; **his** father is also an educator.

567 启动   qǐ dòng   **Verb:** to start; to launch; to switch on

zhè gè xiàng mù yuè dǐ jiù huì qǐ dòng
这个项目月底就会**启动**。
This project will be **launched** at the end of the month.

568 启发   qǐ fā   **Verb:** to inspire
Noun: inspiration

Verb
zài xiě zuò fāng miàn nǐ qǐ fā le wǒ hěn duō
在写作方面，你**启发**了我很多。
In the aspect of writing, you've **inspired** me a lot.

Noun
wǒ hěn gǎn jī yǒu nǐ de qǐ fā hé bāng zhù
我很感激有你的**启发**和帮助。
I am grateful for your **inspiration** and help.

569 启事　　qǐ shì　　**Noun:** notice; announcement

wǒ zài wǎng shàng kàn dào le yì piān xún rén qǐ shì
我 在 网 上 看 到 了 一 篇 寻 人 启 事 。
I saw a missing person **notice** online.

570 起到　　qǐ dào　　**Verb:** to have (effects)

zhè xiē yào duì tā de bìng qǐ dào zuò yòng le ma
这 些 药 对 他 的 病 起 到 作 用 了 吗 ？
Do these medicines **have** any effect on his disease?

571 起码　　qǐ mǎ　　**Adjective:** minimal
　　　　　　　　　　　　　　　　Adverb: at least

Adj.
wǒ yì zhí qī wàng kàn dào qǐ mǎ de xiào guǒ
我 一 直 期 望 看 到 起 码 的 效 果 。
I always expect to see **minimal** results.

Adv.
fàng xīn qǐ mǎ tā xiàn zài bù ké sòu le
放 心 ，起 码 他 现 在 不 咳 嗽 了 。
Don't worry, **at least** he doesn't cough now.

572 气体　　qì tǐ　　**Noun:** gas

qí shí mù xīng shì yí gè qì tǐ xīng qiú
其 实 ， 木 星 是 一 个 气 体 星 球 。
In fact, Jupiter is a **gas** planet.

573 气象　　qì xiàng　　**Noun:** meteorology; weather (formal)

zhāng jiào shòu shì qì xiàng yán jiū de zhuān jiā
张 教 授 是 气 象 研 究 的 专 家 。
Professor Zhang is an expert in **meteorology** (research).

574 签   qiān   **Verb:** to sign

hěn bào qiàn， nín bì xū yòng gāng bǐ qiān
很 抱 歉， 您 必 须 用 钢 笔 签 。
Sorry, you must **sign** with a fountain pen.

575 签订   qiān dìng   **Verb:** to conclude and sign (treaty)

liǎng guó de dài biǎo qiān dìng le mào yì tiáo yuē
两 国 的 代 表 签 订 了 贸 易 条 约 。
Representatives of both countries **signed** a trade treaty.

576 签名   qiān míng   **Verb:** to sign one's name
                                                       Noun: signature

Verb
gē shǒu zài tā de xīn zhuān jí shàng qiān míng le
歌 手 在 他 的 新 专 辑 上 签 名 了 。
The singer **signed his name** on his new album.

Noun
yǒu tā de qiān míng zhēn kù
有 他 的 签 名 真 酷 ！
It's so cool to have his **signature**!

577 签字   qiān zì   **Verb:** to sign (documents)
                                                       Noun: signature

Verb
mì shū huì dài tì zǒng cái zài hé tong shàng qiān zì
秘 书 会 代 替 总 裁 在 合 同 上 签 字 。
The secretary will **sign** the contract on behalf of the CEO.

Noun
duì zhè gè qiān zì yǒu fǎ lǜ xiào lì
对， 这 个 签 字 有 法 律 效 力 。
Yes, this **signature** has legal effect.

578 签约   qiān yuē   **Verb:** to sign a contract

shuāng fāng yuàn yì qiān yuē shí nián
双 方 愿 意 签 约 十 年 。
Both parties are willing **to sign the contract** for 10 years.

579 签证   qiān zhèng   **Noun: visa**

gōng zuò qiān zhèng bǐ lǚ yóu qiān zhèng gèng fù zá
工作签证比旅游签证更复杂。
Work **visas** are more complicated than tourist **visas**.

580 前景   qián jǐng   **Noun: prospect**

zhè suī rán shì xīn gōng sī dàn fā zhǎn qián jǐng hǎo
这虽然是新公司，但发展前景好。
Though it's a new company, it has good development **prospects**.

581 前提   qián tí   **Noun: prerequisite; precondition**

shén me tā gēn nǐ jié hūn de qián tí shì mǎi fáng
什么？她跟你结婚的前提是买房？
What? The **prerequisite** for her to marry you is to buy a house?

582 欠   qiàn   **Verb: to owe**

zhè gè yāo qiú tài guò fèn nǐ gēn běn bú qiàn tā
这个要求太过分，你根本不欠她。
This demand is too much and you don't **owe** her at all.

583 枪   qiāng   **Noun: gun**

wǒ gěi ér zi mǎi le yì bǎ wán jù qiāng
我给儿子买了一把玩具枪。
I bought my son a toy **gun**.

584 强度   qiáng dù   **Noun: intensity; strength (measure)**

yǒu rén shuō diàn nǎo de fú shè qiáng dù hěn qiáng
有人说电脑的辐射强度很强。
Some say that the radiation **intensity** of computers is strong.

585 墙(壁)   qiáng (bì)   **Noun: wall**

bǎ diàn shì guà zài qiáng shàng kě yǐ jié shěng kōng jiān
把 电 视 挂 在 **墙** 上 可 以 节 省 空 间 。
Installing the TV on the **wall** saves space.

zhǐ shì nǐ děi zài qiáng bì shàng dǎ kǒng
只 是 你 得 在 **墙壁** 上 打 孔 。
You just have to drill a hole in the **wall**.

586 抢   qiǎng   **Verb: to rob; to snatch**

tiān a lǎo bǎn de jīn shǒu biǎo zài chē zhàn bèi qiǎng le
天 啊 ！老 板 的 金 手 表 在 车 站 被 **抢** 了 。
Oh god! The boss' gold watch was **snatched** at the station.

587 抢救   qiǎng jiù

Verb: to give emergency treatment
Noun: emergency treatment

Verb
tā bèi sòng dào jí zhěn shì qiǎng jiù le
他 被 送 到 急 诊 室 **抢 救** 了 。
He was taken to the emergency room to receive **emergency treatment**.

Noun
duō kuī yī shēng de qiǎng jiù tā méi yǒu shēng mìng wēi xiǎn
多 亏 医 生 的 **抢 救** ， 他 没 有 生 命 危 险 。
Thanks to the doctor's **emergency treatment**, he is not in a life-threatening condition.

588 强迫   qiǎng pò   **Verb: to force**

dǎi tú yòng dāo qiǎng pò tā tuō xià shǒu biǎo
歹 徒 用 刀 **强 迫** 他 脱 下 手 表 。
The criminal used a knife **to force** him to take off his watch.

589 悄悄　　qiāo qiāo　　**Adverb:** quietly; secretly

huái yùn hòu, tā jiù hé nán yǒu qiāo qiāo jié hūn le
怀孕后，她就和男友**悄悄**结婚了。
After becoming pregnant, she and her boyfriend married **secretly**.

590 敲　　qiāo　　**Verb:** to knock

yǒu rén zài qiāo chuāng, nǐ tīng dào le ma
有人在**敲**窗，你听到了吗？
Someone is **knocking** on the window, do you hear it?

591 敲门　　qiāo mén　　**Verb:** to knock on the door

tā fēng le ma? gàn má bàn yè qiāo mén
他疯了吗？干嘛半夜**敲门**？
Is he crazy? Why **knock on the door** in the middle of the night?

592 瞧　　qiáo　　**Verb:** to take a look (colloquial)

wǒ qù qiáo yi xià, tā kěn dìng zài mèng yóu
我去**瞧**一下，他肯定在梦游。
I'll go **take a look**, he must be sleepwalking.

593 琴　　qín　　**Noun:** zither; general term for stringed musical instruments

wǒ jiā yǒu gāng qín, dà tí qín hé xiǎo tí qín
我家有**钢琴**，**大提琴**和**小提琴**。
I have a **piano**, **cello** and **violin** at home.

594 勤奋　　qín fèn　　**Adjective:** diligent; hardworking

ā xīng hěn qín fèn, liǎng nián hòu jiù shēng zhí le
阿星很**勤奋**，两年后就升职了。
A Xing was **diligent** and was promoted after 2 years.

595 青   qīng   **Adjective:** green; young

zhè shì yì qún xǐ huān qīng sè de qīng shǎo nián
这 是 一 群 喜 欢 青色 的 青少年。
This is a group of teenagers (**young** people) who like **green**.

596 清晨   qīng chén   **Noun:** early morning

wǒ měi tiān qīng chén dōu zuò fēn zhōng de yú jiā
我 每 天 清晨 都 做 20 分 钟 的 瑜 伽。
Every day in the **early morning** I always do 20 minutes of yoga.

597 清理   qīng lǐ   **Verb:** to clear up

wǒ měi zhōu dōu huì huā shí jiān qīng lǐ bàn gōng zhuō
我 每 周 都 会 花 时 间 清理 办 公 桌。
I always spend time **clearing up** my desk every week.

598 情节   qíng jié   **Noun:** plot (movies or stories)

zhè bù diàn yǐng de qíng jié fēi cháng jīng xīn dòng pò
这 部 电 影 的 情节 非 常 惊 心 动 魄。
The **plot** of this movie is very thrilling.

599 情形   qíng xíng   **Noun:** situation

zài jǐn jí qíng xíng xià tā biǎo xiàn de lěng jìng hé guǒ duàn
在 紧 急 情形 下，他 表 现 得 冷 静 和 果 断。
In an emergency **situation**, he remained calm and decisive.

600 晴朗   qíng lǎng   **Adjective:** sunny

jīn tiān tiān qì qíng lǎng shì hé hù wài huó dòng
今 天 天 气 晴朗，适 合 户 外 活 动。
Today's weather is **sunny**, suitable for outdoor activities.

601 区域   qū yù   **Noun:** area; region

shì zhōng xīn yǒu jū zhù qū yù hé shāng yè qū yù
市中心有居住**区域**和商业**区域**。
The city center has residential **areas** and commercial **areas**.

602 全都   quán dōu   **Adverb:** all; without exception

duì yú rì chéng ān pái tā quán dōu jì de
对于日程安排，他**全都**记得。
Regarding the daily schedule, he remembers **all**.

603 全世界   quán shì jiè   **Noun:** worldwide; entire world

quán shì jiè dà gài yǒu duō shǎo rén kǒu
全世界大概有多少人口？
Approximately how many people are there in the **entire world**?

604 泉   quán   **Noun:** spring water; fountain (use with other words)

nǐ zhōu mò xiǎng gēn wǒ qù pào wēn quán ma
你周末想跟我去泡温**泉**吗？
Do you want to go to enjoy the **hot springs** with me this weekend?

605 劝   quàn   **Verb:** to persuade

wǒ quàn ér zi shǎo dǎ yóu xì duō zuò gōng kè
我**劝**儿子少打游戏，多做功课。
I **persuade** my son to play less games and do more homework.

606 缺乏   quē fá   **Verb:** to lack

kě shì tā quē fá jì lù hé xué xí dòng lì
可是他**缺乏**纪律和学习动力。
But he **lacks** discipline and motivation for learning.

607 确立

què lì

Verb: to establish (systems)

què lì xīn jì huà hòu tuán duì xiào lǜ tí shēng le
确 立 新 计 划 后 ， 团 队 效 率 提 升 了 。

After **establishing** the new plan, the team's efficiency increased.

608 群体

qún tǐ

Noun: group

zhè gè shè qū shì yí gè chōng mǎn huó lì de qún tǐ
这 个 社 区 是 一 个 充 满 活 力 的 **群 体** 。

This community is a **group** full of energy.

609 群众

qún zhòng

Noun: people; the masses

zhèng fǔ huān yíng qún zhòng biǎo dá tā men de yì jiàn
政 府 欢 迎 **群 众** 表 达 他 们 的 意 见 。

The government welcomes **people** to express their opinions.

610 染

rǎn

Verb: to dye

wǒ zài kǎo lǜ rǎn fà dàn tā bù tóng yì
我 在 考 虑 **染** 发 ， 但 他 不 同 意 。

I'm thinking about **dyeing** my hair, but he doesn't agree.

611 绕

rào

Verb: to go around; to avoid

tā rào hú qí le yí tàng zì xíng chē
他 **绕** 湖 骑 了 一 趟 自 行 车 。

He took a bike ride **around** the lake.

612 热量

rè liàng

Noun: calories; quantity of heat

tōng guò zhè cì yùn dòng tā xiāo hào le hěn duō rè liàng
通 过 这 次 运 动 ， 他 消 耗 了 很 多 **热 量** 。

Through this exercise, he expended a lot of **calories**.

613 热门

rè mén

Adjective: popular (in great demand)

tā yào rè mén de shǒu jī, bù yào lěng mén de
他 要 **热门** 的 手 机，不 要 冷 门 的。
He wants **popular** phones, not unpopular ones.

614 人间

rén jiān

Noun: human world

zhè běn shū fēn bié miáo xiě le rén jiān hé tiān táng
这 本 书 分 别 描 写 了 **人 间** 和 天 堂。
This book describes the **human world** and heaven respectively.

615 人力

rén lì

Noun: manpower; manual labor

rén gōng zhì néng ràng wǒ men jiǎn shǎo le duì rén lì de yī lài
人 工 智 能 让 我 们 减 少 了 对 **人 力** 的 依 赖。
Artificial intelligence allows us to reduce reliance on **manual labor.**

616 人士

rén shì

Noun: person; individual (prominent)

lǎo bǎn yāo qǐng le shāng yè jiè de zhī míng rén shì
老 板 邀 请 了 商 业 界 的 知 名 **人 士**。
The boss invited famous **individuals** from the business world.

617 人物

rén wù

Noun: character (person)

zhè bù xiǎo shuō de rén wù dōu hěn dú tè
这 部 小 说 的 **人 物** 都 很 独 特。
The **characters** in this novel are all very unique.

618 忍

rěn

Verb: to bear; to tolerate

rú guǒ nǐ yǒu zhè yàng de huài lǎo gōng, nǐ néng rěn ma
如 果 你 有 这 样 的 坏 老 公，你 能 **忍** 吗？
If you had such a bad husband, could you **bear** him?

619 忍不住   rěn bu zhù   **Verb:** unable to bear; cannot help but;

tīng dào tā de gù shì, wǒ rěn bu zhù kū le

听 到 他 的 故 事， 我 忍 不 住 哭 了。

Hearing his story, I **couldn't help but** cry.

---

620 忍受   rěn shòu   **Verb:** to endure

zhè xiē nián tā xué huì le rěn shòu gè zhǒng kùn nán

这 些 年 他 学 会 了 忍 受 各 种 困 难。

Over the years he learned **to endure** all kinds of hardships.

---

621 认   rèn   **Verb:** to recognize

tīng shuō shā rén fàn zài fǎ tíng shàng rèn zuì le

听 说 杀 人 犯 在 法 庭 上 认 罪 了。

I heard that the murderer confessed (**recognize** crime) in court.

---

622 认定   rèn dìng   **Verb:** to identify; to confirm

jǐng chá shàng zhōu rèn dìng le xián yí rén de shēn fèn

警 察 上 周 认 定 了 嫌 疑 人 的 身 份。

Police **identified** (the identity of) the suspect last week.

---

623 扔   rēng   **Verb:** to throw

shén me? tā yì shōu dào qíng shū jiù rēng le

什 么？ 她 一 收 到 情 书 就 扔 了？

What? She **threw** away the love letter as soon as she received it?

---

624 仍旧   réng jiù   **Adverb:** still

méi xiǎng dào tā réng jiù nà me wú qíng

没 想 到 她 仍 旧 那 么 无 情 ！

I didn't expect she is **still** so heartless!

625 如此   rú cǐ   **Pronoun:** such; so; in this way

rú cǐ   méi rén gǎn zài zhǔ dòng zhuī qiú tā le

如此，没人敢再主动追求她了。

In this way, no one dares to actively pursue her anymore.

626 如同   rú tóng   **Verb:** as; like

nǐ de xiào róng rú tóng yáng guāng   wēn nuǎn ér míng liàng

你的笑容**如同**阳光，温暖而明亮。

Your smile is **like** sunshine, warm and bright.

627 如下   rú xià   **Verb:** as follows; as below

bù zhòu rú xià   xiān fù zhì   zài zhān tiē

步骤**如下**：先复制，再粘贴。

The steps are **as follows**: first copy, then paste.

628 入门   rù mén   **Verb:** to start learning; to learn the basics

tā de jí tā hái méi yǒu rù mén

他的吉他还没有**入门**。

He hasn't **learnt the basics** of guitar.

629 软   ruǎn   **Adjective:** soft

zhè zhāng chuáng de diàn zi hěn ruǎn   fēi cháng shū shì

这张床的垫子很**软**，非常舒适。

The mattress on this bed is **soft** and very comfortable.

630 软件   ruǎn jiàn   **Noun:** software

gōng sī de ruǎn jiàn xiāo shòu chāo guò le yìng jiàn

公司的**软件**销售超过了硬件。

The company's **software** sales exceed hardware sales.

631 洒 — să

Verb: to spill; to sprinkle

wǒ bù xiǎo xīn bǎ mài piàn zhōu să zài le dì shàng
我 不 小 心 把 麦 片 粥 洒 在 了 地 上 。

I accidentally **spilled** my cereal on the floor.

632a 散 — săn

Verb: to come loose; to fall apart

zāo gāo wǒ de zhǐ xiāng săn le
糟 糕 ！ 我 的 纸 箱 散 了 。

Oops! My carton **fell apart**.

632b 散 — sàn

Verb: to scatter; to disperse

fēng chuī sàn le shù shàng de yè zi
风 吹 散 了 树 上 的 叶 子 。

The wind blew and **scattered** the leaves on the trees.

633 散文 — săn wén

Noun: prose

tā shàn cháng xiě shī wǒ shàn cháng xiě săn wén
她 擅 长 写 诗 ， 我 擅 长 写 散 文 。

She's good at writing poetry, I'm good at writing **prose**.

634 杀 — shā

Verb: to kill

jù shuō tā zài zhàn chǎng shàng shā le jiǔ gè rén
据 说 他 在 战 场 上 杀 了 九 个 人 。

He is said to have **killed** 9 men on the battlefield.

635 杀毒 — shā dú

Verb: to kill virus

yì bān de jiǔ jīng kě yǐ shā dú ma
一 般 的 酒 精 可 以 杀 毒 吗 ？

Can regular alcohol **kill viruses**?

636 沙漠　　shā mò　　**Noun:** desert

沙漠的气候太干燥，植物很少。
shā mò de qì hòu tài gān zào，zhí wù hěn shǎo

The **desert** climate is too dry; so there are few plants.

637 傻　　shǎ　　**Adjective:** silly; foolish

他看上去很傻，其实很精明。
tā kàn shàng qù hěn shǎ，qí shí hěn jīng míng

He looks **foolish**, but he is actually very shrewd.

638 山区　　shān qū　　**Noun:** mountainous area

是他开发了这片山区的矿石。
shì tā kāi fā le zhè piàn shān qū de kuàng shí

It was he that developed the minerals in this **mountainous area**.

639a 扇　　shān　　**Verb:** to flutter; to slap; to flap;

不管怎样，别扇别人的脸。
bù guǎn zěn yàng，bié shān bié rén de liǎn

No matter what, don't **slap** people in the face.

639b 扇　　shàn　　**Classifier** for fan, window, door

我想在新家安装一扇木门。
wǒ xiǎng zài xīn jiā ān zhuāng yí shàn mù mén

I want to install a wooden door in my new home.

640 扇子　　shàn zi　　**Noun:** fan

这扇子上是她亲手画的山水画。
zhè shàn zi shàng shì tā qīn shǒu huà de shān shuǐ huà

On this **fan** is a landscape painting drawn by herself.

641 商标
shāng biāo

Noun: logo; trademark

ér qiě shàng miàn yě yǒu tā de qiān míng hé shāng biāo
而且上面也有她的签名和**商标**。
And it also has her signature and **logo** on it.

642 上级
shàng jí

Noun: superior

wǒ zài xié tiáo shàng jí hé xià jí de gōng zuò
我在协调**上级**和下级的工作。
I'm coordinating the work of **superiors** and subordinates.

643 上下
shàng xià

Noun: the whole; up and down

bǎo chí gōng sī shàng xià tuán jié hěn zhòng yào
保持公司**上下**团结很重要。
It's important to keep **the whole** company united.

644 上涨
shàng zhǎng

Verb: to rise; to go up

tōng huò péng zhàng ràng wù jià shàng zhǎng le
通货膨胀让物价**上涨**了！
Inflation makes products' prices **rise**!

645 稍
shāo

Adverb: a bit (use with other words)

qǐng nǐ men shāo děng dài biǎo tuán mǎ shàng jiù dào
请你们**稍**等，代表团马上就到。
Please **wait a bit**, the delegation will arrive shortly.

646 稍微
shāo wēi

Adverb: slightly

wǒ fā xiàn zhāng zǒng shāo wēi yǒu xiē bú nài xīn
我发现张总**稍微**有些不耐心。
I have noticed that Director Zhang is **slightly** impatient.

647 蛇

shé

Noun: snake

nǐ kàn, cǎo cóng zhōng yǒu yì wō shé dàn
你 看，草 丛 中 有 一 窝 **蛇 蛋**。
Look, there's a nest of **snake** eggs in the grass.

648 舍不得

shě bu de

Verb: reluctant to part with or use (out of care)

wǒ mā shě bu de huā dà qián mǎi xīn shā fā
我 妈 **舍 不 得** 花 大 钱 买 新 沙 发。
My mom is **reluctant to** spend a lot of money on a new sofa.

649 舍得

shě de

Verb: not begrudge; be willing to part with

dàn shì wǒ bà shě de, yīn wèi tā de gōng zī gāo
但 是 我 爸 **舍 得**，因 为 他 的 工 资 高。
But my dad **doesn't begrudge** to do so, as he earns a high salary.

650 设想

shè xiǎng

Verb: to imagine
Noun: tentative idea

Verb
shè xiǎng nǐ de nián xīn shì yì bǎi wàn, nǐ huì zěn me zuò
设 想 你 的 年 薪 是 一 百 万，你 会 怎 么 做？
Imagine your annual salary is 1 million, what would you do?

Noun
zhè gè shè xiǎng hěn yòu rén, dàn bú xiàn shí
这 个 **设 想** 很 诱 人，但 不 现 实。
This **idea** is tempting, but unrealistic.

651 社

shè

Noun: society; group (use with other words)

wǒ de guī mì zài yì jiā guó jì lǚ xíng shè gōng zuò
我 的 闺 蜜 在 一 家 国 际 **旅 行 社** 工 作。
My best friend works at an international **travel group**.

652 社区   shè qū   **Noun:** community

tā hé wǒ dōu shì wǒ men shè qū de zhì yuàn zhě
她 和 我 都 是 我 们 **社 区** 的 志 愿 者 。
She and I are both volunteers in our **community**.

653 射   shè   **Verb:** to shoot; to send/shoot out (light)

zhè hái zi xǐ huān yòng shuǐ qiāng shè bié rén zhēn tiáo pí
这 孩 子 喜 欢 用 水 枪 **射** 别 人 ， 真 调 皮 ！
This child likes **to shoot** others with a water gun, so naughty!

wǔ tái shàng shè chū le wǔ yán liù sè de dēng guāng
舞 台 上 **射** 出 了 五 颜 六 色 的 灯 光 。
Colorful lights are **shooting out** from the stage.

654 射击   shè jī   **Verb:** to shoot; to fire

yě xǔ tā huì dāng bīng xué xí zhuān yè shè jī
也 许 他 会 当 兵 ， 学 习 专 业 **射 击** 。
Perhaps he'll be a soldier and learn **to shoot** professionally.

655 摄像   shè xiàng   **Verb:** to undertake videography

zuì jìn wǒ nán péng yǒu zài xué xí zhuān yè shè xiàng
最 近 我 男 朋 友 在 学 习 专 业 **摄 像** 。
Recently, my boyfriend is studying professional **videography**.

656 摄像机   shè xiàng jī   **Noun:** video camera

tā huā le liǎng qiān měi jīn mǎi le yí gè xīn shè xiàng jī
他 花 了 两 千 美 金 买 了 一 个 新 **摄 像 机** 。
He spent 2000 US dollars to buy a new **video camera**.

657 摄影

shè yǐng

Verb: to undertake photography; (professional)

zhè fèn xīn gōng zuò shì wèi míng xīng hé mó tè shè yǐng
这 份 新 工 作 是 为 明 星 和 模 特 **摄 影**。
This new job is for **photographing** celebrities and models.

658 摄影师

shè yǐng shī

Noun: photographer; cameraman

wǒ men xū yào zhāo pìn yǒu jīng yàn de shè yǐng shī
我 们 需 要 招 聘 有 经 验 的 **摄 影 师**。
We need to hire experienced **photographers**.

659 伸

shēn

Verb: to stretch

shǒu jī diào xià qù de shí hòu wǒ shēn shǒu qù zhuā
手 机 掉 下 去 的 时 候， 我 **伸** 手 去 抓。
When the phone fell down, I **stretched** my hand to catch it.

660 深处

shēn chù

Noun: deep area; profundity

kě shì wǒ méi zhuā zhù tā diào jìn le hú de shēn chù
可 是 我 没 抓 住， 它 掉 进 了 湖 的 **深 处**。
But I didn't catch it, and it fell into the **deep area** of the lake.

661 深度

shēn dù

Noun: depth; deepness

tīng shuō zhè gè hú de píng jūn shēn dù shì sān shí mǐ
听 说 这 个 湖 的 平 均 **深 度** 是 三 十 米。
I heard that the average **depth** of this lake is 30 meters.

662 神

shén

Noun: god; divinity; spirit

yǒu xiē rén xìn shén dàn shì bú xìn zōng jiào
有 些 人 信 **神**， 但 是 不 信 宗 教。
Some people believe in **God**, but do not believe in religion.

663 神经

shén jīng

Noun: nerve

kǒng pà tā yǒu shén jīng bìng de qīng xiàng

恐 怕 他 有 **神 经** 病 的 倾 向 。

I'm afraid that he has a tendency towards insanity (**nerve** disease).

664 神奇

shén qí

Adjective: magical; miraculous; wondrous

zhè gè mó shù shī de mó shù kàn qǐ lái hěn shén qí

这 个 魔 术 师 的 魔 术 看 起 来 很 **神 奇** 。

This magician's magic appears very **mircaulous**.

665 神情

shén qíng

Noun: expression (look of eyes)

měi gè guān zhòng de shén qíng dōu hěn jīng yà

每 个 观 众 的 **神 情** 都 很 惊 讶 。

The **expressions** of every audience member were very amazed.

666 升高

shēng gāo

Verb: to raise; to lift; to escalate

dǎo yǎn shuō yào xiǎng bàn fǎ shēng gāo wǔ tái

导 演 说 要 想 办 法 **升 高** 舞 台 。

The director said we need to find a way **to raise** the stage.

667 生成

shēng chéng

Verb: to generate; to produce
Noun: generation

Verb

zhè gè ruǎn jiàn kě yǐ shēng chéng cái wù zhàng dān

这 个 软 件 可 以 **生 成** 财 务 账 单 。

This software can **generate** financial invoices.

Noun

zhè xiē shù jù de shēng chéng zhǐ yào wǔ fēn zhōng

这 些 数 据 的 **生 成** 只 要 五 分 钟 。

The **generation** of this data only takes 5 minutes.

668 声　　　shēng　　　**Noun:** sound; voice

zhè gè gù shì de lù yīn xū yào nán shēng hé nǚ shēng
这 个 故 事 的 录 音 需 要 男 **声** 和 女 **声**。
The recording for this story requires both male and female **voices**.

669 胜负　　　shèng fù　　　**Noun:** victory and defeat

qí shí　zhàn zhēng de shèng fù hěn nán yù liào
其 实， 战 争 的 **胜 负** 很 难 预 料。
Actually, it's hard to predict **victory and defeat** of war.

670 剩(下)　　　shèng (xià)　　　**Verb:** be left over; to remain

jiāng jūn tóu xiáng hòu　shèng xià de shì bīng chè tuì le
将 军 投 降 后， **剩 下** 的 士 兵 撤 退 了。
After the general surrendered, the **remaining** soldiers retreated.

wǒ bù xǐ huān làng fèi　yě bú jiè yì chī shèng fàn
我 不 喜 欢 浪 费， 也 不 介 意 吃 **剩** 饭。
I don't like waste and don't mind eating **left over** food.

671 失误　　　shī wù　　　**Noun:** error

rèn hé rén dōu huì fàn cuò　shī wù shì cháng jiàn de
任 何 人 都 会 犯 错， **失 误** 是 常 见 的。
Anyone can make mistakes; **errors** are common.

672 师傅　　　shī fu　　　**Noun:** master (polite term to address male worker)

zhāng shī fu　nín de ān zhuāng gōng zuò yào duō jiǔ
张 **师 傅**， 您 的 安 装 工 作 要 多 久 ？
Master Zhang, how long will your installation work take?

673 诗歌

shī gē

Noun: poem; poetry

zhè shǒu gǔ diǎn **shī gē** yòu yōu měi yòu làng màn
这 首 古 典 **诗 歌** 又 优 美 又 浪 漫 。

This classical **poem** is both beautiful and romantic.

674 十足

shí zú

Adjective: full; sheer; 100 percent

zhè gè shī rén yí dìng shì yí wèi **shí zú** de tiān cái
这 个 诗 人 一 定 是 一 位 **十 足** 的 天 才 。

This poet must be a **sheer** genius.

675 时常

shí cháng

Adverb: often

dāng nián wǒ men **shí cháng** yì qǐ qù dà hǎi yóu yǒng
当 年 我 们 **时 常** 一 起 去 大 海 游 泳 。

Back then we **often** went to the sea to swim together.

676 时光

shí guāng

Noun: time (poetic)

nà shì wǒ tóng nián shí dài zuì kuài lè de **shí guāng**
那 是 我 童 年 时 代 最 快 乐 的 **时 光** 。

That was the happiest **time** of my childhood era.

677 时机

shí jī

Noun: opportunity

bú yào cuò guò zhè yàng zhēn guì de **shí jī**
不 要 错 过 这 样 珍 贵 的 **时 机** 。

Don't miss such a precious **opportunity**.

678 时事

shí shì

Noun: current affairs

tā guān xīn **shí shì** sī xiǎng yě xiān jìn
他 关 心 **时 事** ， 思 想 也 先 进 。

He cares about **current affairs** and has progressive ideas.

679 实惠 shí huì

Adjective: substantial; good deal; bargain
Noun: material benefit

Adj.
zhè gè píng bǎn pián yi, zhì liàng yě hǎo, zhēn shí huì
这 个 平 板 便 宜 ， 质 量 也 好 ， 真 实 惠 。
This tablet is cheap and of good quality, a real **bargain**.

Noun
gù kè dé dào le shí huì jiù huì gěi hǎo píng
顾 客 得 到 了 实 惠 就 会 给 好 评 。
Customers will give good reviews when they get **benefits**.

680 拾 shí

Verb: to pick up (things)

wǒ men qù shā tān shí bàng ké, zěn me yàng
我 们 去 沙 滩 拾 蚌 壳 ， 怎 么 样 ?
How about we go to the beach **to pick up** clam shells?

681 使得 shǐ de

Verb: to make; to cause
Adjective: usable; workable

Verb
tā de huà shǐ de wǒ yì zhěng tiān dōu yù mèn
他 的 话 使 得 我 一 整 天 都 郁 闷 。
His words **caused** me to be depressed all day long.

Adj.
zhè gè jiàn pán yòu lǎo yòu pò, hái shǐ de ma
这 个 键 盘 又 老 又 破 ， 还 使 得 吗 ?
This keyboard is old and broken, is it still **usable**?

682 示范 shì fàn

Verb: to demonstrate
Noun: demonstration

Verb
kōng jiě zài gěi wǒ men shì fàn chuān jiù shēng yī
空 姐 在 给 我 们 示 范 穿 救 生 衣 。
The stewardess is **demonstrating** to us how to put on life jackets.

Noun
tā de shì fàn hěn yǒu yòng, wǒ jì zhù le
她 的 示 范 很 有 用 ， 我 记 住 了 。
Her **demonstration** is helpful and I've remembered it.

683 式   shì   **Noun:** type; style; pattern (use with other words)

^{wǒ} 我 ^{men} 们 ^{zài} 在 ^{guǎng} 广 ^{zhōu} 州 ^{jǔ} 举 ^{bàn} 办 ^{le} 了 ^{shèng} 盛 ^{dà} 大 ^{de} 的 ^{zhōng} **中** ^{shì} **式** ^{hūn} 婚 ^{lǐ} 礼 。

We held a grand **Chinese-style** wedding in Guangzhou.

684 势力   shì lì   **Noun:** power (of influence)

^{zǒng} 总 ^{tǒng} 统 ^{shì} 是 ^{shì} 世 ^{jiè} 界 ^{shàng} 上 ^{zuì} 最 ^{yǒu} 有 ^{shì} **势** ^{lì} **力** ^{de} 的 ^{rén} 人 ^{ma} 吗 ？

Is the president the most **power**ful man in the world?

685 试图   shì tú   **Verb:** to attempt; to try to

^{tā} 他 ^{céng} 曾 ^{shì} **试** ^{tú} **图** ^{yǔ} 与 ^{wǒ} 我 ^{men} 们 ^{qiān} 签 ^{dìng} 订 ^{hé} 和 ^{píng} 平 ^{xié} 协 ^{yì} 议 。

He previously **attempted** to make a peace agreement with us.

686 视频   shì pín   **Noun:** video

^{tā} 他 ^{shì} 试 ^{tú} 图 ^{shān} 删 ^{chú} 除 ^{shì} **视** ^{pín} **频** ， ^{dàn} 但 ^{chǒu} 丑 ^{wén} 闻 ^{hái} 还 ^{shì} 是 ^{bào} 曝 ^{guāng} 光 ^{le} 了 。

He tried to delete the **video**, but the scandal still came to light.

687 视为   shì wéi   **Verb:** to be seen as; to regard as

^{yé} 耶 ^{sū} 稣 ^{bèi} 被 ^{shì} **视** ^{wéi} **为** ^{wěi} 伟 ^{dà} 大 ^{de} 的 ^{zhěng} 拯 ^{jiù} 救 ^{zhě} 者 。

Jesus is **regarded as** the great savior.

688 收购   shōu gòu   **Verb:** to purchase; to acquire

^{gōng} 公 ^{sī} 司 ^{bèi} 被 ^{shōu} **收** ^{gòu} **购** ^{hòu} 后 ， ^{lǐng} 领 ^{dǎo} 导 ^{céng} 层 ^{huàn} 换 ^{rén} 人 ^{le} 了 。

After the company was **acquired**, the leadership team was replaced.

689 收集　　　shōu jí　　　**Verb:** to collect

wǒ ér zi xǐ huān shōu jí gè guó de yóu piào
我儿子喜欢**收集**各国的邮票。
My son likes **to collect** stamps from various countries.

690 收拾　　　shōu shi　　　**Verb:** to pack; to tidy up

míng tiān jiù yào qù dù jià le kuài diǎn shōu shi xíng li
明天就要去度假了，快点**收拾**行李。
We're going on vacation tomorrow, **pack** your bags quickly.

691 手段　　　shǒu duàn　　　**Noun:** trick; means; measure

tā shǒu duàn gāo míng shì bàn gōng shì zhèng zhì de gāo shǒu
他**手段**高明，是办公室政治的高手。
He has great **tricks** and is a master of office politics.

692 手法　　　shǒu fǎ　　　**Noun:** technique (manual method)

zhè zhǒng cì xiù shǒu fǎ hěn jīng xì bù róng yì xué
这种刺绣**手法**很精细，不容易学。
This embroidery **technique** is delicate and not easy to learn.

693 寿司　　　shòu sī　　　**Noun:** sushi

tā gěi wǒ zuò le yì pán shòu sī hé yì wǎn shòu miàn
她给我做了一盘**寿司**和一碗寿面。
She made me a plate of **sushi** and a bowl of longevity noodles.

694 受灾　　　shòu zāi　　　**Verb:** to be hit by disaster

wǒ men zài wèi shòu zāi rén qún juān zèng wù zī
我们在为**受灾**人群捐赠物资。
We are donating supplies to people **hit by the disaster**.

695 瘦　　shòu　　**Adjective:** slim; thin

tā yǒu diǎn shòu ， zhǐ yǒu sì shí liù gōng jīn
她 有 点 **瘦** ， 只 有 四 十 六 公 斤 。
She is a little **thin**, only forty-six kilograms.

696 书法　　shū fǎ　　**Noun:** calligraphy

wǒ xǐ huān liàn shū fǎ ， tā xǐ huān liàn jiàn fǎ
我 喜 欢 练 **书 法** ， 他 喜 欢 练 剑 法 。
I like to practice **calligraphy**; he likes to practice swordsmanship.

697 书柜　　shū guì　　**Noun:** bookcase

tā zài shū guì lǐ cáng le yí wàn yīng bàng de xiàn jīn
他 在 **书 柜** 里 藏 了 一 万 英 镑 的 现 金 。
He hid £10,000 in cash in a **bookcase**.

698 书桌　　shū zhuō　　**Noun:** writing desk

yào shi zài shū zhuō de dì yī céng chōu ti lǐ
钥 匙 在 **书 桌** 的 第 一 层 抽 屉 里 。
The key is in the first drawer of the **writing desk**.

699 输出　　shū chū　　**Verb:** to output; to export

wǒ shū rù mì mǎ ， diàn nǎo xiǎn shì shū chū cuò wù
我 输 入 密 码 ， 电 脑 显 示 **输 出** 错 误 。
I input the password, and the computer displayed an **output** error.

700 蔬菜　　shū cài　　**Noun:** vegetables

wǒ gǔ lì hái zi duō chī shuǐ guǒ hé shū cài
我 鼓 励 孩 子 多 吃 水 果 和 **蔬 菜** 。
I encourage my children to eat more fruits and **vegetables**.

701 熟悉

shú xī

Verb: be familiar
Adjective: familiar

Verb

wǒ de gǒu duì zhōu wéi de huán jìng hěn shú xī
我 的 狗 对 周 围 的 环 境 很 熟 悉 。
My dog **is familiar** with the surrounding environment.

Adj.

tā zǒng néng yòng bí zi xiù dào shú xī de wèi dào
它 总 能 用 鼻 子 嗅 到 熟 悉 的 味 道 。
It can always smell a **familiar** scent with its nose.

702 鼠

shǔ

Noun: mouse; rat

hěn duō zhōng guó rén jué de shǔ nián bú tài jí lì
很 多 中 国 人 觉 得 鼠 年 不 太 吉 利 。
Many Chinese feel that the Year of the **Rat** isn't very auspicious.

703 鼠标

shǔ biāo

Noun: computer mouse

zāo gāo wǒ de shǔ biāo bèi kā fēi nòng zāng le
糟 糕 ！ 我 的 鼠 标 被 咖 啡 弄 脏 了 。
Oops! My **mouse** got dirty from coffee.

704 数目

shù mù

Noun: number; amount

yù suàn de shù mù tài dà zǒng cái huì tóng yì ma
预 算 的 数 目 太 大 ， 总 裁 会 同 意 吗 ？
The budget **amount** is too big; will the CEO agree?

705 摔

shuāi

Verb: to throw; to break

shén me tā bǎ bēi zi shuāi zài le dì shàng
什 么 ？ 他 把 杯 子 摔 在 了 地 上 ？
What? He **threw** the cup to the floor?

706 摔倒

shuāi dǎo   **Verb:** to fall down

tā bù xiǎo xīn cǎi dào le xiāng jiāo pí， yě shuāi dǎo le
他不小心踩到了香蕉皮，也**摔倒**了。

He accidentally stepped on a banana peel and **fell down** too.

707 率领

shuài lǐng   **Verb:** to lead

wáng zǒng jiān shuài lǐng wǒ men bù mén wán chéng le rèn wù
王总监**率领**我们部门完成了任务。

Director Wang **led** our department to complete the task.

708 双手

shuāng shǒu   **Noun:** both hands; pair of hands

nǐ cāi tā shuāng shǒu bào zhe de lǐ wù shì shén me
你猜他**双手**抱着的礼物是什么？

Can you guess what gift he is holding in his **hands**?

709 水产品

shuǐ chǎn pǐn   **Noun:** aquatic product

zhè xiē shuǐ chǎn pǐn shì yǒu míng de guǎng dōng tè chǎn
这些**水产品**是有名的广东特产。

These **aquatic products** are famous Guangdong specialties.

710 水分

shuǐ fèn   **Noun:** water content; moisture

xī guā de shuǐ fèn gāo， kě yǐ jiě kě
西瓜的**水分**高，可以解渴。

Watermelon has a high **water content**, which can quench thirst.

711 水库

shuǐ kù   **Noun:** reservoir

shuǐ kù dà gài yǒu èr shí duō gè gōng zuò rén yuán
水库大概有二十多个工作人员。

There are probably more than 20 workers at the **reservoir**.

712 水灾   shuǐ zāi   **Noun:** flood; inundation

xiāng bǐ shuǐ zāi   huǒ zāi gèng kě pà
相 比 **水 灾**， 火 灾 更 可 怕。
Compared to **floods**, fire disaster is more horrible.

713 睡眠   shuì mián   **Noun:** sleep; slumber

chī ān mián yào zhēn de kě yǐ tí gāo shuì mián ma
吃 安 眠 药 真 的 可 以 提 高 **睡 眠** 吗？
Can taking sleeping pills really improve **sleep**?

714 说法   shuō fǎ   **Noun:** saying; statement; wording

tā de shuō fǎ yǒu diǎn piàn miàn   bù kě xìn
他 的 **说 法** 有 点 片 面， 不 可 信。
His **statement** is a bit one-sided and untrustworthy.

715 硕士   shuò shì   **Noun:** Master's (postgraduate degree)

wǒ nǚ péng yǒu zài qīng huá dà xué dú shuò shì
我 女 朋 友 在 清 华 大 学 读 **硕 士**。
My girlfriend is studying a **Master's** at Tsinghua University.

716 私人   sī rén   **Adjective:** personal; private

tā yǒu sī rén zhù sù hé yán jiū shì
她 有 **私 人** 住 宿 和 研 究 室。
She has **private** accommodation and a research room.

717 思维   sī wéi   **Noun:** thinking

wǒ men zài duì bǐ xíng xiàng sī wéi hé chōu xiàng sī wéi
我 们 在 对 比 形 象 **思 维** 和 抽 象 **思 维**。
We are contrasting figurative **thinking** with abstract **thinking**.

718 四周　　sì zhōu　　**Noun:** all around

jǐng chá zài sì zhōu jiǎn chá kě yí de wù pǐn
警察在**四周**检查可疑的物品。
Police were looking **all around** for suspicious items.

719 搜　　sōu　　**Verb:** to search

tā men sōu dào le yí gè zhuāng zhe zhà dàn de hēi dài zi
他们**搜**到了一个装着炸弹的黑袋子。
They found (by **searching**) a black bag with a bomb inside.

720 搜索　　sōu suǒ　　**Verb:** to search for (information)

nǐ kě yǐ zài wǎng shàng sōu suǒ jù tǐ xìn xī
你可以在网上**搜索**具体信息。
You can **search for** specific information online.

721 宿舍　　sù shè　　**Noun:** dormitory

wǒ men sù shè yǒu gè tǎo yàn de shì yǒu
我们**宿舍**有个讨厌的室友。
We have an annoying roommate in our **dormitory**.

722 酸甜苦辣　　suān tián kǔ là　　**Noun:** joys and sorrows; sour, sweet, bitter, spicy

rú guǒ méi yǒu suān tián kǔ là shēng huó jiù tài kū zào le
如果没有**酸甜苦辣**，生活就太枯燥了。
If people didn't have **joys and sorrows**, life would be too boring.

723 随后　　suí hòu　　**Adverb:** shortly; soon afterwards

qǐng dà jiā xiān rù chǎng zhǔ chí rén suí hòu jiù dào
请大家先入场，主持人**随后**就到。
Please enter first, the host will arrive **shortly**.

724 随意   suí yì   **Adjective:** random; casual

dì yī cì yuē huì de shí hòu shuō huà bú yào tài suí yì

第一次约会的时候，说话不要太**随意**。

On a first date, don't be too **casual** with your conversation.

725 随着   suí zhe   **Preposition:** as; along with

suí zhe shí jiān de tuī yí nǐ men huì gèng liǎo jiě duì fāng

随着时间的推移，你们会更了解对方。

As time goes by, you will get to know each other better.

726 岁月   suì yuè   **Noun:** years/time (poetic)

suì yuè de hén jì shì nǐ men gǎn qíng de jiàn zhèng

岁月的痕迹是你们感情的见证。

The traces of **time** are witnesses of your relationship.

727 碎   suì   **Verb:** to break

fēn shǒu hòu tā gǎn jué xīn suì le lā hēi le wǒ

分手后她感觉心**碎**了，拉黑了我。

After the breakup, she felt heart**broken** and blocked me.

728 损害   sǔn hài   **Verb:** to harm; to damage
Noun: damage

Verb

xìng chǒu wén sǔn hài le lǎo bǎn de míng shēng

性丑闻**损害**了老板的名声。

Sex scandal **damaged** the boss' reputation.

Noun

zhè xiē sǔn hài bú shì jīn qián kě yǐ jì suàn de

这些**损害**不是金钱可以计算的。

These **damages** cannot be measured in terms of money.

729 损失　　　sǔn shī

Noun: loss
(from damage)

tā zāo shòu le jīng jì **sǔn shī** hé jīng shén **sǔn shī**
他 遭 受 了 经 济 **损 失** 和 精 神 **损 失**。
He suffered financial **loss** as well as emotional **losses**.

730 所在　　　suǒ zài

Noun: place;
location; cause

wǒ men bì xū zhǎo dào wèn tí de **suǒ zài** cái néng
我 们 必 须 找 到 问 题 的 **所 在** 才 能
jiě jué tā
解 决 它 。
We have to find the **cause** of the problem in order to solve it.

731 锁　　　suǒ

Verb: to lock
Noun: lock

Verb
chū mén de shí hòu qiān wàn jì de **suǒ** mén
出 门 的 时 候 ， 千 万 记 得 **锁** 门 。
When you go out, you must remember **to lock** the door.

Noun
zhè bǎ zhì néng **suǒ** yǒu yǔ yīn gōng néng
这 把 智 能 **锁** 有 语 音 功 能 。
This smart **lock** has voice functionality.

732 台风　　　tái fēng

Noun: typhoon

dāng dì jū mín zǒng shì zāo shòu **tái fēng** de qīn rǎo
当 地 居 民 总 是 遭 受 **台 风** 的 侵 扰 。
Local residents always suffer from the disturbances of **typhoons**.

733 抬　　　tái

Verb: to carry;
to lift (heavy things)

má fán nǐ men bāng wǒ bǎ shā fā **tái** dào kè tīng
麻 烦 你 们 帮 我 把 沙 发 **抬** 到 客 厅 。
May I trouble you to help **carry** the sofa to the living room.

734 抬头　tái tóu　**Verb:** to look up; to raise one's head

抬头 表示自信，低头表示自卑。
tái tóu biǎo shì zì xìn，dī tóu biǎo shì zì bēi

Raising one's head indicates confidence; lowering it indicates a lack of confidence.

735 太空　tài kōng　**Noun:** space (universe)

只有少数人尝试过**太空**旅游。
zhǐ yǒu shǎo shù rén cháng shì guò tài kōng lǚ yóu

Only a minority of people have tried **space** travel.

736 弹　tán　**Verb:** to flick; to play; to leap

我会**弹**吉他，但不会**弹**钢琴。
wǒ huì tán jí tā，dàn bú huì tán gāng qín

I can **play** the guitar, but can't **play** the piano.

737 逃　táo　**Verb:** to escape

新闻上说有个犯人从监狱**逃**了。
xīn wén shàng shuō yǒu gè fàn rén cóng jiān yù táo le

The news said that a prisoner **escaped** from the prison.

738 逃跑　táo pǎo　**Verb:** to run away

他**逃跑**得太快，警察没追上。
tā táo pǎo de tài kuài，jǐng chá méi zhuī shàng

He **ran away** too fast for the police to catch up.

739 逃走　táo zǒu　**Verb:** to flee

听说他已经**逃走**了，现在在国外。
tīng shuō tā yǐ jīng táo zǒu le，xiàn zài zài guó wài

I heard that he has **fled** and is now abroad.

740 桃　　táo　　**Noun:** peach

wǒ ài chī táo ， hèn chī lí ， nǐ ne ？
我 爱 吃 **桃**， 恨 吃 梨， 你 呢 ？
I love eating **peaches** but hate eating pears, what about you?

741 桃花　　táo huā　　**Noun:** peach blossom

wǒ xǐ huān táo huā ， yīng huā ， lán huā hé méi guī huā 。
我 喜 欢 **桃 花**， 樱 花， 兰 花 和 玫 瑰 花 。
I like **peach blossoms**, cherry blossoms, orchids and roses.

742 桃树　　táo shù　　**Noun:** peach tree

zhè lǐ yǒu táo shù 、 lí shù 、 píng guǒ shù děng děng 。
这 里 有 **桃 树**、 梨 树、 苹 果 树 等 等 。
Here are **peach trees**, pear trees, apple trees and so on.

743 讨厌　　tǎo yàn　　**Verb:** to dislike
Adjective: annoying

Verb
tóng xué men ài xué xí ， dàn shì tǎo yàn kǎo shì 。
同 学 们 爱 学 习， 但 是 **讨 厌** 考 试 。
Classmates love studying, but **dislike** taking exams.

Adj.
nà gè lǎo shī tài luō suo ， yǒu diǎn tǎo yàn 。
那 个 老 师 太 啰 嗦， 有 点 **讨 厌** 。
That teacher is too talkative and a bit **annoying**.

744 特定　　tè dìng　　**Adjective:** specially given/appointed

yì xiē nèi gé guān yuán shì shǒu xiàng tè dìng de 。
一 些 内 阁 官 员 是 首 相 **特 定** 的 。
Some cabinet officials are **specifically appointed** by the Prime Minister.

745 特性   tè xìng   **Noun:** feature; characteristic

zhè kuǎn shǒu jī de **tè xìng** dú tè ， shì hé nǐ
这 款 手 机 的 **特 性** 独 特 ， 适 合 你 。
This mobile phone has unique **features**, suitable for you.

746 特有   tè yǒu   **Adjective:** typical; peculiar

ér qiě ， zhè xiàng gōng néng shì pǐn pái **tè yǒu** de
而 且 ， 这 项 功 能 是 品 牌 **特 有** 的 。
Moreover, this function is brand-**typical**.

747 提倡   tí chàng   **Verb:** to advocate

wǒ men **tí chàng** bǎo hù huán jìng ， jiǎn shǎo qì tǐ wū rǎn
我 们 **提 倡** 保 护 环 境 ， 减 少 气 体 污 染 。
We **advocate** for protecting the environment and reducing air pollution.

748 提起   tí qǐ   **Verb:** to mention; to speak of

měi cì **tí qǐ** wǒ de qián rèn ， wǒ dōu jué de fán
每 次 **提 起** 我 的 前 任 ， 我 都 觉 得 烦 ！
Every time someone **mentions** my ex, I get annoyed!

749 提示   tí shì   **Verb:** to remind; to point out   **Noun:** hint

Verb
nǐ zuì hǎo **tí shì** tā shǎo wèn zhè zhǒng wèn tí
你 最 好 **提 示** 他 少 问 这 种 问 题 。
You'd better **remind** him to ask less questions like this.

Noun
fàng xīn ba ， wǒ yí dìng huì gěi tā **tí shì** de
放 心 吧 ， 我 一 定 会 给 他 **提 示** 的 。
Don't worry, I will definitely give him a **hint**.

750 题材

tí cái

Noun: subject theme

guān yú xiǎo shuō， wǒ duì shén huà tí cái zuì gǎn xìng qù
关 于 小 说， 我 对 神 话 题 材 最 感 兴 趣。

Regarding fiction, I'm most interested in mythological **themes**.

751 体积

tǐ jī

Noun: bulk;
volume (size of container)

xiāng zi de tǐ jī tài dà， fàng bù jìn wǒ de chē
箱 子 的 体 积 太 大， 放 不 进 我 的 车。

The **volume** of this box is too large to fit in my car.

752 体力

tǐ lì

Noun: physical
strength/energy

zài shuō， tái zhè me duō xiāng zi hěn xiāo hào tǐ lì
再 说， 抬 这 么 多 箱 子 很 消 耗 体 力。

Besides, carrying so many boxes takes a lot of **energy**.

753 天才

tiān cái

Noun: genius

wǒ yǐ qián jué de tā shì tiān cái， xiàn zài fā xiàn shì
我 以 前 觉 得 他 是 天 才， 现 在 发 现 是
chǔn cái
蠢 材。

I used to think he was a **genius**, but now I realize he is a fool.

754 天然气

tiān rán qì

Noun: natural gas

zhè jiā gōng sī shì quán guó zuì dà de tiān rán qì
这 家 公 司 是 全 国 最 大 的 天 然 气
gōng yìng shāng
供 应 商。

The company is the largest **natural gas** supplier in the country.

755 天文

tiān wén

Noun: astronomy

wǒ ér zi duì shù xué tiān wén hé dì lǐ yǒu xìng qù
我儿子对数学、**天文**和地理有兴趣。
My son's interested in mathematics, **astronomy** and geography.

756 调节

tiáo jié

Verb: to adjust;
to regulate

wǒ yào qǐng rén tiáo jié zhè gè jiè zhǐ de chǐ cùn
我要请人**调节**这个戒指的尺寸。
I need to pay someone **to adjust** the size of this ring.

757 调解

tiáo jiě

Verb: to mediate

lǜ shī zài bāng tā men tiáo jiě shāng wù jiū fēn
律师在帮他们**调解**商务纠纷。
Lawyers are helping them **mediate** business disputes.

758 厅

tīng

Noun: hall; room

wǒ jiā de fàn tīng hé kè tīng shì lián jiē de
我家的饭**厅**和客**厅**是连接的。
My dining **room** and living **room** are connected.

759 停留

tíng liú

Verb: to stay
(temporarily)

zhè cì chū chāi wǒ dǎ suàn zài ào mén tíng liú yì zhōu
这次出差，我打算在澳门**停留**一周。
For this business trip, I plan **to stay** in Macau for a week.

760 通用　　tōng yòng

Verb: to be interchangeable
Adjective: universal; general-purpose

Verb
zhè liǎng gè duǎn yǔ kě yǐ tōng yòng
这 两 个 短 语 可 以 **通 用** 。
These two phrases can **be interchangeable**.

Adj.
zhè zhǒng chōng diàn qì shì tōng yòng de shì hé gè zhǒng shǒu jī
这 种 充 电 器 是 **通 用** 的 ，适 合 各 种 手 机 。
This charger is **universal** and suitable for all kinds of mobiles.

761 偷　　tōu

Verb: to steal

nà gè xiǎo tōu kuài sù de tōu le tā de qián bāo
那 个 小 偷 快 速 地 **偷** 了 她 的 钱 包 。
The thief quickly **stole** her purse.

762 偷偷　　tōu tōu

Adverb: stealthily; secretly

rán hòu tā tōu tōu de shàng le gōng jiāo chē
然 后 ， 他 **偷 偷** 地 上 了 公 交 车 。
Then he **secretly** got on the bus.

763 突破　　tū pò

Verb: to breakthrough
Noun: breakthrough

Verb
jì shù yuán men yì qǐ tū pò le zhè gè nán tí
技 术 员 们 一 起 **突 破** 了 这 个 难 题 。
The technicians worked together **to break through** this problem.

Noun
zhè gè ruǎn jiàn shì gōng sī de jì shù tū pò
这 个 软 件 是 公 司 的 技 术 **突 破** 。
The software is the company's technological **breakthrough**.

764 土豆　　　　tǔ dòu　　　　**Noun:** potato

tā huì zuò tǔ dòu tiáo、tǔ dòu ní hé tǔ dòu bǐng
他会做**土豆**条、**土豆**泥和**土豆**饼。
He makes **potato** chips, mashed **potatoes** and **potato** pies.

765a 吐　　　　tǔ　　　　**Verb:** to spit; to pour out

kě xī zhè bēi jiǔ tài nán hē，wǒ tǔ le
可惜这杯酒太难喝，我**吐**了。
Unfortunately, this wine is so unpleasant that I **spat** it out.

765b 吐　　　　tù　　　　**Verb:** to vomit

tā hē le tài duō pí jiǔ，xiàn zài shàng tù xià xiè
他喝了太多啤酒，现在上**吐**下泻。
He drank too much beer and now is **vomiting** and having diarrhea.

766 兔　　　　tù　　　　**Noun:** rabbit; hare

yuè shén cháng é de chǒng wù shì yì zhī tù zi
月神嫦娥的宠物是一只**兔**子。
The pet of the Moon Goddess Chang'e is a **rabbit**.

767 团长　　　　tuán zhǎng　　　　**Noun:** commander; head of a delegation

tuán zhǎng zài yàn huì shàng hē zuì le，kàn shàng qù hěn gān gà
团长在宴会上喝醉了，看上去很尴尬！
The **head** was drunk at the party and looked embarrassed!

768 推行　　　　tuī xíng　　　　**Verb:** to carry out; to implement

zhèng fǔ míng nián sì yuè huì tuī xíng xīn de shuì wù zhèng cè
政府明年四月会**推行**新的税务政策。
The government will **implement** new tax policies next April.

769 脱离 tuō lí

Verb: to break away from

为了**脱离**控制，一些公司去国外了。
wèi le tuō lí kòng zhì，yì xiē gōng sī qù guó wài le

To break away from control, some companies went abroad.

770 外界 wài jiè

Noun: outside (external world)

除了个人烦恼，他还要承受**外界**压力。
chú le gè rén fán nǎo，tā hái yào chéng shòu wài jiè yā lì

Except personal troubles, he also has to endure **outside** pressure.

771 完了 wán le

Phrase: be over; come to an end

看来问题太多，他的事业**完了**！
kàn lái wèn tí tài duō，tā de shì yè wán le

It seems that he has too many issues; his career is **over**!

772 微博 wēi bó

Noun: Weibo (Chinese social media app)

这个明星在**微博**上有两千万粉丝。
zhè gè míng xīng zài wēi bó shàng yǒu liǎng qiān wàn fěn sī

This movie star has 20 million followers on **Weibo**.

773 为难 wéi nán

Verb: to make something difficult
Adjective: difficult (feeling)

Verb

他借钱不还，故意**为难**我。
tā jiè qián bù huán，gù yì wéi nán wǒ

He borrows money yet refuses to repay it, deliberately **making things difficult** for me.

Adj.

我该不该让他还钱呢？真**为难**！
wǒ gāi bù gāi ràng tā huán qián ne？zhēn wéi nán

Should I ask him to pay back the money? How **difficult**!

774 为期

wéi qī

Adverb: latest by (date)

dāng rán ràng tā jǐn kuài huán qián ， **wéi qī** liǎng gè yuè
当 然 让 他 尽 快 还 钱 ， **为 期** 两 个 月 。
Of course let him pay back the money soon, **latest by** 2 months.

775 为止

wéi zhǐ

Adverb: by; till; up to

rú guǒ jiǔ yuè **wéi zhǐ** tā hái bù xíng dòng ， jiù gào tā
如 果 九 月 **为 止** 他 还 不 行 动 ， 就 告 他 。
If **by** September he still doesn't act, sue him.

776 为主

wéi zhǔ

Verb: to put something first

tā bù yīng gāi zǒng shì yǐ zì jǐ de lì yì **wéi zhǔ**
他 不 应 该 总 是 以 自 己 的 利 益 **为 主** 。
He should not always **put first** his own interests .

777 违法

wéi fǎ

Adjective: illegal

fàn mài dú pǐn zài xīn jiā pō shì yán zhòng **wéi fǎ** de
贩 卖 毒 品 在 新 加 坡 是 严 重 **违 法** 的 。
The sale of drugs in Singapore is seriously **illegal**.

778 违反

wéi fǎn

Verb: to violate

zhèng fǔ yán gé dǎ jī **wéi fǎn** fǎ lǜ de rén
政 府 严 格 打 击 **违 反** 法 律 的 人 。
The government takes strict action against those who **violate** the law.

779 违规

wéi guī

Verb: to violate rules

lǎo wáng zài gōng sī **wéi guī** dǔ bó ， bèi chǎo le
老 王 在 公 司 **违 规** 赌 博 ， 被 炒 了 。
Wang **violated** rules by gambling in the company and was fired.

780 围绕 wéi rào **Verb:** to surround

zhè gè hú wéi rào zhe shān gǔ , měi jí le
这 个 湖 **围 绕** 着 山 谷 ， 美 极 了 ！

The lake **surrounds** the valley, so stunning!

781 唯一 wéi yī **Adjective:** only

zhè lǐ shì wéi yī ràng wǒ gǎn dào píng jìng de dì fāng
这 里 是 **唯 一** 让 我 感 到 平 静 的 地 方 。

This is the **only** place where I feel calm.

782 委托 wěi tuō **Verb:** to entrust

tā wěi tuō lǜ shī zài tā sǐ hòu wèi tā fēn pèi
她 **委 托** 律 师 在 她 死 后 为 她 分 配
cái chǎn
财 产 。

She **entrusted** a lawyer to distribute her wealth after her death.

783 卫星 wèi xīng **Noun:** satellite

xī chāng shì zhōng guó yǒu míng de wèi xīng fā shè zhōng xīn
西 昌 是 中 国 有 名 的 **卫 星** 发 射 中 心 。

Xichang is China's famous **satellite** launch center.

784 胃 wèi **Noun:** stomach

yǒu rén shuō bù chī zǎo fàn duì wèi bù hǎo
有 人 说 不 吃 早 饭 对 **胃** 不 好 。

Some people say that not eating breakfast is bad for the **stomach**.

785 慰问　wèi wèn

Verb: to send warm greetings
Noun: condolences; warm greetings

Verb
qǐng dài wǒ wèi wèn nǐ de xiōng dì jiě mèi
请 代 我 慰 问 你 的 兄 弟 姐 妹 。
Please **send** my **warm greetings** to your brothers and sisters.

Noun
kǎ piàn shàng xiě de shì tā de wèi wèn hé zhù fú
卡 片 上 写 的 是 他 的 慰 问 和 祝 福 。
The card contains his **warm greetings** and wishes.

786 温和　wēn hé

Adjective: gentle; mild

tā de xìng gé yòu wēn hé yòu qiān xū
他 的 性 格 又 温 和 又 谦 虚 ！
His personality is **gentle** and humble!

787 文艺　wén yì

Noun: literature and art

zài wén yì fāng miàn tā yě yǒu cái huá
在 文 艺 方 面 ， 他 也 有 才 华 。
In the aspect of **literature and art**, he's also talented.

788 卧室　wò shì

Noun: bedroom

wǒ de wò shì zì dài wèi shēng jiān fēi cháng fāng biàn
我 的 卧 室 自 带 卫 生 间 ， 非 常 方 便 。
My **bedroom** has its own bathroom, which is very convenient.

789 握　wò

Verb: to hold; to grasp

tā de shǒu lǐ jǐn jǐn wò zhe bā bǎi yuán hóng bāo
他 的 手 里 紧 紧 握 着 八 百 元 红 包 。
He was tightly **holding** a red envelope with ¥800 in his hand.

790 污染　　wū rǎn

Verb: to pollute
Noun: pollution

Verb

zhè gè gōng chǎng de fèi shuǐ wū rǎn le huán jìng
这 个 工 厂 的 废 水 **污 染** 了 环 境 。
The wastewater from this factory **pollutes** the environment.

Noun

yóu yú wū rǎn yán zhòng lǎo bǎn bèi fá le yì bǎi wàn yuán
由 于 **污 染** 严 重 ， 老 板 被 罚 了 一 百 万 元 。
Due to serious **pollution**, the boss was fined 1 million yuan.

791 污水　　wū shuǐ　　**Noun:** polluted water

yǒu xiào de chǔ lǐ zhè xiē wū shuǐ shì shǒu yào rèn wù
有 效 地 处 理 这 些 **污 水** 是 首 要 任 务 。
Effective treatment of this **polluted water** is a top priority.

792 屋　　wū

Noun: room;
small house

méi huā lín lǐ yǒu yì jiān gǔ diǎn xiǎo mù wū
梅 花 林 里 有 一 间 古 典 小 木 **屋** 。
There is a classic wooden **house** in the plum blossom forest.

793 无奈　　wú nài

Adjective: helpless;
choiceless
Conjunction: however;
unfortunately

Adj.

duì yú fēn shǒu wǒ men dōu gǎn jué hěn wú nài
对 于 分 手 ， 我 们 都 感 觉 很 **无 奈** 。
About the breakup, we both feel **helpless**.

Conj.

wǒ men suī rán hái zài hu duì fāng wú nài bú ài le
我 们 虽 然 还 在 乎 对 方 ， **无 奈** 不 爱 了 。
Although we still care about each other, **unfortunately** we do not love.

794 无疑　　wú yí　　**Adverb:** undoubtedly

shuō shí huà zhè wú yí shì zhèng què de xuǎn zé
说 实 话 ， 这 **无 疑** 是 正 确 的 选 择 。
To be honest, this is **undoubtedly** the right choice.

795 舞　　　wǔ　　　**Noun:** dance

tā men tiào de bā lěi wǔ fēi cháng jīng yàn
她 们 跳 的 芭 蕾 舞 非 常 惊 艳 。
The ballet (**dance**) they danced was amazing.

796 物价　　　wù jià　　　**Noun:** price (commodity)

wù jià shàng zhǎng ràng wǒ men de shēng huó jié jū
物 价 上 涨 让 我 们 的 生 活 拮 据 。
Rising prices have made our lives frugal.

797 物业　　　wù yè　　　**Noun:** property (houses)

wù yè guǎn lǐ fèi yòng shì měi nián sān bǎi měi yuán
物 业 管 理 费 用 是 每 年 三 百 美 元 。
The **property** management fee is $300 per year.

798 物质　　　wù zhì　　　**Noun:** material

wǒ ài zhuī qiú jīng shén xiǎng shòu bú shì wù zhì xiǎng shòu
我 爱 追 求 精 神 享 受 ， 不 是 物 质 享 受 。
I love to pursue spiritual enjoyment, not **material** enjoyment.

799 误解　　　wù jiě　　　**Verb:** to misunderstand　**Noun:** misunderstanding

Verb
qí shí nǐ men wù jiě tā de yì si le
其 实 你 们 误 解 她 的 意 思 了 。
In fact, you have **misunderstood** her.

Noun
wǒ qīng chǔ zhè jiàn shì kě yǐ bāng nǐ men jiě chú wù jiě
我 清 楚 这 件 事 ， 可 以 帮 你 们 解 除 误 解 。
I'm aware of this matter and can help you resolve the **misunderstanding**.

800 西红柿　　xī hóng shì　　**Noun:** tomato

xī hóng shì yòu jiào fān qié, wéi shēng sù C hán liàng gāo
西红柿又叫番茄，维生素C含量高。
Tomatoes, also called "fan qie", are high in vitamin C.

801 西装　　xī zhuāng　　**Noun:** suit (western-style)

wǒ gěi lǎo gōng dìng zuò le yí tào xī zhuāng
我给老公定做了一套**西装**。
I had a **suit** made for my husband.

802 喜剧　　xǐ jù　　**Noun:** comedy

tā shì běi měi zhōu zuì chū míng de xǐ jù yǎn yuán zhī yī
他是北美洲最出名的**喜剧**演员之一。
He is one of North America's most famous **comedy** actors.

803 戏　　xì　　**Noun:** playful act; trick; play (performance)

bié zài wǒ miàn qián zuò xì, wǒ shòu bu liǎo
别在我面前做**戏**，我受不了！
Don't play **tricks** in front of me, I can't stand it!

804 戏剧　　xì jù　　**Noun:** drama (performance)

wǒ jiàn yì nǐ qù kàn zhuān yè de xì jù biǎo yǎn
我建议你去看专业的**戏剧**表演。
I suggest you go see a professional **drama** performance.

805 吓　　xià　　**Verb:** to scare

wǒ de māo tiào de tài gāo, xià le wǒ de xiǎo gǒu
我的猫跳得太高，**吓**了我的小狗。
My cat jumped too high and **scared** my puppy.

806 先后 — xiān hòu — **Adverb:** successively; one after another

míng xīng men zài fěn sī de huān hū zhōng xiān hòu rù chǎng le
明星们在粉丝的欢呼中**先后**入场了。
Celebrities entered the venue **one after another** amid cheers from fans.

807 先前 — xiān qián — **Noun:** beforehand; previously

xiān qián tā men zhōng de hěn duō rén dōu zǒu guò hóng tǎn
先前他们中的很多人都走过红毯。
Previously many of them have walked the red carpet.

808 鲜艳 — xiān yàn — **Adjective:** bright and colorful

zǒu zài zhè xiān yàn de dì tǎn shàng hěn xiǎng shòu
走在这**鲜艳**的地毯上很享受。
Walking on this **bright and colorful** carpet is enjoyable.

809 闲 — xián — **Adjective:** idle; unoccupied

wǒ wài gōng tuì xiū le rì zi guò de hěn xián
我外公退休了，日子过得很**闲**。
My grandpa is retired and has a very **idle** life.

810 显 — xiǎn — **Verb:** to show; to appear

tā méi shén me ài hào xiǎn de hěn wú liáo
他没什么爱好，**显**得很无聊。
He doesn't have any hobbies and **appears** very bored.

811 现有 — xiàn yǒu — **Adjective:** existing

xiǎo qū xiàn yǒu de yú lè chǎng suǒ zài nǎ lǐ
小区**现有**的娱乐场所在哪里？
Where are the **existing** entertainment venues in the community?

812 现状　xiàn zhuàng　**Noun:** present situation

nián qīng rén de shī yè xiàn zhuàng ràng rén dān yōu
年 轻 人 的 失 业 **现 状** 让 人 担 忧 。

The **present situation** of unemployment among young people is worrying.

813 线索　xiàn suǒ　**Noun:** clue

zhè chǎng móu shā àn jiàn yǒu xiàn suǒ le ma
这 场 谋 杀 案 件 有 **线 索** 了 吗 ？

Are there any **clues** to this murder case?

814 献　xiàn　**Verb:** to offer; to present

yǒu gè cōng míng de shì bīng gěi jiāng jūn xiàn jì le
有 个 聪 明 的 士 兵 给 将 军 **献** 计 了 。

A clever soldier **presented** a scheme to the general.

815 乡　xiāng　**Noun:** rural area (use with other words)

jì móu shì zài xiāng jiān gěi dí rén shè mái fu
计 谋 是 在 **乡** 间 给 敌 人 设 埋 伏 。

The strategy is to set up an ambush for the enemy in the **rural area**.

816 乡村　xiāng cūn　**Noun:** village; countryside

zhè gè xiāng cūn de rén kǒu dà gài shì yì qiān rén
这 个 **乡 村** 的 人 口 大 概 是 一 千 人 。

The population of this **village** is about 1000 people.

817 相等　xiāng děng　**Verb:** to equal

zhè liǎng píng jiǔ de jiǔ jīng hán liàng bù xiāng děng
这 两 瓶 酒 的 酒 精 含 量 不 **相 等** 。

The alcohol content of the two bottles of wine is not **equal**.

818 相应   xiāng yìng

Verb: to correspond
Adjective: corresponding

Verb
gù shì de kāi tóu hé jié wěi yīng gāi xiāng yìng
故 事 的 开 头 和 结 尾 应 该 **相 应** 。
The beginning and end of the story should **correspond**.

Adj.
miàn duì jì zhě de tí wèn tā gěi le xiāng yìng de huí dá
面 对 记 者 的 提 问 ，他 给 了 **相 应** 的 回 答 。
Faced with reporters' questions, he gave **corresponding** answers.

819 香肠   xiāng cháng

Noun: sausage

wǒ zuì ài de xiǎo chī shì sì chuān xiāng cháng chǎo fàn
我 最 爱 的 小 吃 是 四 川 **香 肠** 炒 饭 。
My favorite snack is Sichuan **sausage** fried rice.

820 详细   xiáng xì

Adjective: detailed

tā bǎ gù shì qíng jié miáo shù de hěn xiáng xì
他 把 故 事 情 节 描 述 得 很 **详 细** 。
He described a very **detailed** storyline.

821 享受   xiǎng shòu

Verb: to enjoy
Adjective: enjoyable

Verb
guò lái hé wǒ yì qǐ xiǎng shòu zhè gè gù shì ba
过 来 和 我 一 起 **享 受** 这 个 故 事 吧 。
Come to **enjoy** this story with me.

Noun
yì biān tīng yì biān hē chá zuì xiǎng shòu
一 边 听 一 边 喝 茶 最 **享 受** 。
It's most **enjoyable** to drink tea while listening.

822 向导   xiàng dǎo

Noun: guide (person)

tàn xiǎn duì de xiàng dǎo yǒu fēng fù de jīng yàn
探 险 队 的 **向 导** 有 丰 富 的 经 验 。
The expedition **guide** has rich experience.

823 向前   xiàng qián   **Verb:** forward; onward

bù guǎn yù dào shén me kùn nán, jì de xiàng qián kàn

不管遇到什么困难，记得**向前**看。

No matter what difficulties you encounter, remember to look **forward**.

824 向上   xiàng shàng   **Verb:** upward; up

zài xiàng shàng pá èr shí mǐ, wǒ men jiù dào zhōng diǎn le

再**向上**爬二十米，我们就到终点了。

Climb **upward** another 20 meters and we'll reach the end.

825 相声   xiàng sheng   **Noun:** crosstalk

wǒ de yí gè běi jīng lǎo péng yǒu shì xiàng sheng yǎn yuán

我的一个北京老朋友是**相声**演员。

An old friend of mine in Beijing is a **crosstalk** actor.

826 象征   xiàng zhēng   **Verb:** to symbolize   **Noun:** symbol

Verb

jié hūn jiè zhǐ xiàng zhēng yì shēng de ài yǔ chéng nuò

结婚戒指**象征**一生的爱与承诺。

Wedding rings **symbolize** a life of love and commitment.

Noun

zhè gè lǐ wù shì wǒ men gǎn qíng de xiàng zhēng

这个礼物是我们感情的**象征**。

This gift is a **symbol** of our relationship.

827 消除   xiāo chú   **Verb:** to eliminate

xǐ shǒu yè kě yǐ bāng zhù xiāo chú xì jūn

洗手液可以帮助**消除**细菌。

Hand sanitizer can help **eliminate** germs.

828 消毒　　xiāo dú　　**Verb:** to disinfect

duì le, jiǔ jīng yě kě yǐ xiāo dú ma
对 了， 酒 精 也 可 以 **消 毒** 吗 ？
By the way, can alcohol **disinfect**?

829 消防　　xiāo fáng　　**Noun:** fire fighting

wǒ yào dǎ diàn huà gěi xiāo fáng rén yuán jiù huǒ
我 要 打 电 话 给 **消 防** 人 员 救 火 。
I need to call the **fire fighting** men to put out the fire.

830 消费者　　xiāo fèi zhě　　**Noun:** consumer

zhè shì yà zhōu shì chǎng de xiāo fèi zhě diào chá bào gào
这 是 亚 洲 市 场 的 **消 费 者** 调 查 报 告 。
This is a **consumer** survey report on the Asian market.

831 消极　　xiāo jí　　**Adjective:** negative (attitude)

duō shù rén jī jí, shǎo shù rén xiāo jí
多 数 人 积 极， 少 数 人 **消 极** 。
The majority of people are positive; the minority are **negative**.

832 小偷　　xiǎo tōu　　**Noun:** thief

shén me? xiǎo tōu jū rán shì yí gè yùn fù
什 么？ **小 偷** 居 然 是 一 个 孕 妇 ？
What? The **thief** is actually a pregnant woman?

833 歇　　xiē　　**Verb:** to rest (use with other words)

zǒu le yí gè xiǎo shí le, wǒ yào zuò xià xiē jiǎo
走 了 一 个 小 时 了， 我 要 坐 下 **歇** 脚 。
After walking for an hour, I need to sit down **to rest** my **feet**.

834 协议   xié yì   **Noun:** agreement

<small>lǎo bǎn ràng wǒ jǐn kuài cǎo nǐ yí gè xié yì</small>
老 板 让 我 尽 快 草 拟 一 个 **协 议** 。
My boss asked me to draft an **agreement** as soon as possible.

835 协议书   xié yì shū   **Noun:** written agreement

<small>liǎng fāng dài biǎo děi zài xié yì shū shàng qiān zì</small>
两 方 代 表 得 在 **协 议 书** 上 签 字 。
Representatives of both parties must sign the **written agreement**.

836 斜   xié   **Verb:** to slant; to turn sideways; **Adjective:** oblique; slanted

Verb
<small>zhuō zi xié le zán men bǎ tā fú zhèng</small>
桌 子 **斜** 了 ， 咱 们 把 它 扶 正 。
The table is **slanting**, let's straighten it.

Adj.
<small>zhè zhǒng shū fǎ zì tǐ yǒu diǎn xié</small>
这 种 书 法 字 体 有 点 **斜** 。
This calligraphy font is a bit **slanted**.

837 心态   xīn tài   **Noun:** mentality

<small>bǎo chí lè guān de xīn tài hěn zhòng yào</small>
保 持 乐 观 的 **心 态** 很 重 要 。
It's important to maintain a positive **mentality**.

838 心疼   xīn téng   **Verb:** to care deeply (have strong empathy)

<small>wǒ xīn téng mǔ qīn xiǎng bāng tā zǎo diǎn tuì xiū</small>
我 **心 疼** 母 亲 ， 想 帮 她 早 点 退 休 。
I **care for** my mother **deeply** and want to help her retire early.

839 辛苦 xīn kǔ

Verb: to work hard; to suffer (courteous)
Adjective: hard; laborious

Verb
您 一 路 辛 苦 了 ！
nín yí lù xīn kǔ le
I appreciate you had a long journey (a road of **suffering**)!

Adj
晚 上 加 班 很 辛 苦！
wǎn shàng jiā bān hěn xīn kǔ
Working overtime at night is **hard**!

840 欣赏 xīn shǎng

Verb: to appreciate (out of admiration)

我 很 欣 赏 你 的 才 华 和 决 心 。
wǒ hěn xīn shǎng nǐ de cái huá hé jué xīn
I **appreciate** your talent and determination.

841 信念 xìn niàn

Noun: belief

耶 稣 的 爱 是 我 坚 实 的 信 念 。
yé sū de ài shì wǒ jiān shí de xìn niàn
The love of Jesus is my firm **belief**.

842 信箱 xìn xiāng

Noun: mailbox; letter box

我 的 信 箱 里 有 太 多 广 告 信 件 。
wǒ de xìn xiāng lǐ yǒu tài duō guǎng gào xìn jiàn
There are too many advertising letters in my **mailbox**.

843 行驶 xíng shǐ

Verb: to go; to fly; to travel (vehicles)

海 上 有 轮 船 和 快 艇 在 行 驶 。
hǎi shàng yǒu lún chuán hé kuài tǐng zài xíng shǐ
There are ships and speedboats **traveling** on the sea.

844 形态　　　xíng tài　　　**Noun:** form

shuǐ kě yǐ cóng yè tǐ **xíng tài** zhuǎn wéi qì tǐ **xíng tài**
水 可 以 从 液 体 **形 态** 转 为 气 体 **形 态** 。
Water can change from liquid **form** to gas **form**.

845 性能　　　xìng néng　　　**Noun:** function

zhè tái diàn nǎo de **xìng néng** yòu qí quán yòu qiáng dà
这 台 电 脑 的 **性 能** 又 齐 全 又 强 大 。
The **function** of this computer is complete and powerful.

846 雄伟　　　xióng wěi　　　**Adjective:** majestic; magnificent

zì yóu nǚ shén xiàng shì yí zuò **xióng wěi** de diāo xiàng
自 由 女 神 像 是 一 座 **雄 伟** 的 雕 像 。
The Statue of Liberty is a **majestic** statue.

847 熊　　　xióng　　　**Noun:** bear

dòng wù yuán lǐ yǒu **xióng** dàn méi yǒu xióng māo
动 物 园 里 有 **熊** ， 但 没 有 熊 猫 。
There are **bears** in the zoo, but no pandas.

848 休闲　　　xiū xián　　　**Noun:** leisure　**Adjective:** relaxing

Noun
zài **xiū xián** shí jiān wǒ xǐ huān qù jiàn shēn fáng
在 **休 闲** 时 间 ， 我 喜 欢 去 健 身 房 。
In my **leisure** time, I like to go to the gym.

Adj
tā de tuì xiū shēng huó hěn **xiū xián**
她 的 退 休 生 活 很 **休 闲** 。
Her retirement life is **relaxing**.

849 修复   xiū fù   **Verb:** to repair; to restore

zhè xiē bì huà tuō luò le hěn duō xū yào xiū fù
这 些 壁 画 脱 落 了 很 多 ， 需 要 修 复 。
The mural has peeled off a lot and needs to be **restored**.

850 修建   xiū jiàn   **Verb:** to build

wǒ men kě yǐ zài tā zhōu wéi xiū jiàn fáng hù lán
我 们 可 以 在 它 周 围 修 建 防 护 栏 。
We can **build** a protective fence around it.

851 修养   xiū yǎng   **Verb:** to recuperate

chū yuàn hòu tā qù le xià wēi yí xiū yǎng
出 院 后 ， 他 去 了 夏 威 夷 修 养 。
After being discharged from the hospital, he went to Hawaii **to recuperate**.

852 虚心   xū xīn   **Adjective:** humble; modest
Noun: humility; modesty

Adj.
tā yòu xū xīn yòu shàng jìn fēi cháng shòu huān yíng
他 又 虚 心 又 上 进 ， 非 常 受 欢 迎 。
He is **humble** and progressive, so very popular.

Noun
xū xīn shì tā zuì dà de rén gé mèi lì
虚 心 是 他 最 大 的 人 格 魅 力 。
Humility is his greatest personality charm.

853 许可 xǔ kě

Verb: to allow; to permit
Noun: permission

Verb
只要条件**许可**，就可以尝试。
zhǐ yào tiáo jiàn xǔ kě jiù kě yǐ cháng shì
As long as conditions **permit**, you can try it.

Noun
项目资金已经获得了总裁的**许可**。
xiàng mù zī jīn yǐ jīng huò dé le zǒng cái de xǔ kě
Project funding **permission** has been obtained from the president.

854 选修 xuǎn xiū

Verb: to take as an elective (academic)

我朋友建议我**选修**书法和美术。
wǒ péng yǒu jiàn yì wǒ xuǎn xiū shū fǎ hé měi shù
My friend suggested that I **take** calligraphy and fine art **as electives**.

855 学科 xué kē

Noun: discipline; subject

财务会计是我们学院很火的**学科**。
cái wù kuài jì shì wǒ men xué yuàn hěn huǒ de xué kē
Financial accounting is a very popular **subject** in our college.

856 学位 xué wèi

Noun: degree (academic)

我估计明年六月能拿到**学位**证书。
wǒ gū jì míng nián liù yuè néng ná dào xué wèi zhèng shū
I estimate that I will get my **degree** certificate next June.

857 学者 xué zhě

Noun: scholar; man of learning

对于真正的**学者**，学习没有尽头。
duì yú zhēn zhèng de xué zhě xué xí méi yǒu jìn tóu
For a true **scholar**, there is no end to learning.

858 寻求

xún qiú

Verb: to look for; to seek; to explore

tā men bú huì tíng zhǐ xún qiú xīn de zhī shi hé tiǎo zhàn
他们不会停止**寻求**新的知识和挑战。
They'll never stop **seeking** new knowledge and challenges.

859 询问

xún wèn

Verb: to inquire

wǒ yào xiàng rén shì bù mén xún wèn yǎng lǎo jīn de wèn tí
我要向人事部门**询问**养老金的问题。
I want **to inquire** about pension issues from the HR department.

860 押金

yā jīn

Noun: deposit

wǒ mǎi fáng de yā jīn shì wǔ wàn měi yuán
我买房的**押金**是五万美元。
The **deposit** I put on my house was 50,000 dollars.

861 鸭子

yā zi

Noun: duck

wǒ jīng yà de fā xiàn yě yā zi huì fēi
我惊讶地发现野**鸭子**会飞。
I was surprised to find that wild **ducks** could fly.

862 亚军

yà jūn

Noun: runner-up

tīng shuō guàn jūn hé yà jūn dōu shì měi guó rén
听说冠军和**亚军**都是美国人。
I heard that the champion and **runner-up** are both American.

863 延伸

yán shēn

Verb: to extend

zhè zuò qiáo yì zhí yán shēn dào hé de duì àn
这座桥一直**延伸**到河的对岸。
The bridge **extends** to the other side of the river.

864 严厉   yán lì   **Adjective:** severe (strictness)

zuì fàn bì xū jiē shòu yán lì de fǎ lù chéng fá
罪 犯 必 须 接 受 **严 厉** 的 法 律 惩 罚 。
Criminals must accept **severe** legal punishment.

865 严肃   yán sù   **Adjective:** serious (attitude)

fǎ guān fēi cháng yán sù bó huí le tā de sù sòng
法 官 非 常 **严 肃** ， 驳 回 了 他 的 诉 讼 。
The judge was very **serious** and dismissed his lawsuit.

866 言语   yán yǔ   **Noun:** words; speech; parole

tā de yán yǔ hěn wēn róu wēn nuǎn le wǒ de xīn
他 的 **言 语** 很 温 柔 ， 温 暖 了 我 的 心 。
His **words** were so gentle and warmed my heart.

867 研究所   yán jiū suǒ   **Noun:** research institute

yán jiū suǒ yí gòng yǒu shí wèi jīng jì xué zhuān jiā
研 究 所 一 共 有 十 位 经 济 学 专 家 。
The **research institute** has ten economics experts.

868 眼光   yǎn guāng   **Noun:** vision; insight; perspective

tā men dà duō yǎn guāng dú tè cái huá héng yì
他 们 大 多 **眼 光** 独 特 ， 才 华 横 溢 。
Most of them have unique **insights** and abundant talent.

869 邀请　yāo qǐng

Verb: to invite
Noun: invitation

Verb

wǒ xiǎng yāo qǐng tā men cān jiā zhè jiè de shāng wù lùn tán
我 想 **邀 请** 他 们 参 加 这 届 的 商 务 论 坛 。
I want **to invite** them to attend this business forum.

Noun

qǐng nǐ gěi tā men yī yī fā sòng yāo qǐng hán
请 你 给 他 们 一 一 发 送 **邀 请** 函 。
Please send **invitation** letters to them one by one.

870 摇头　yáo tóu

Verb:
to shake one's head

qǐng kuài diǎn huí dá nǐ kě yǐ diǎn tóu huò yáo tóu
请 快 点 回 答 ，你 可 以 点 头 或 **摇 头** 。
Please answer quickly, you can nod or **shake** your **head**.

871 咬　yǎo

Verb: to bite

shén me nǐ tóng xué de pì gǔ bèi shé yǎo le
什 么 ？你 同 学 的 屁 股 被 蛇 **咬** 了 ？
What? Your classmate got **bitten** by a snake on the butt?

872 也好　yě hǎo

Phrase: may as well;
also works fine

tā bù lái yě hǎo bù rán dà jiā kě néng huì xiào tā
他 不 来 **也 好** ，不 然 大 家 可 能 会 笑 他 。
He **may as well** not come, otherwise people might laugh at him.

873 业务　yè wù

Noun: service
(business)

wǒ men gōng sī tí gōng de shì gāo duān jīn róng yè wù
我 们 公 司 提 供 的 是 高 端 金 融 **业 务** 。
Our company provides high-end financial **services**.

874 夜间

yè jiān

Noun: nighttime; at night

nǎ pà zài **yè jiān** ， kè fú yě huì zài xiàn huí fù nín
哪 怕 在 **夜 间** ， 客 服 也 会 在 线 回 复 您 。

Even **at night**, customer service will respond to you online.

875 一流

yī liú

Adjective: first-rate; top-notch

jiàn lì **yī liú** de pǐn pái shi wǒ men de mù biāo
建 立 **一 流** 的 品 牌 是 我 们 的 目 标 。

Building a **first-rate** brand is our goal.

876 依法

yī fǎ

Adverb: according to the law

hěn duō zhèng kè méi yǒu **yī fǎ** shǐ yòng quán lì
很 多 政 客 没 有 **依 法** 使 用 权 力 。

Many politicians do not use their power **according to the law**.

877 依旧

yī jiù

Adverb: still

tā men zhōng de yì xiē guān yuán **yī jiù** fǔ bài
他 们 中 的 一 些 官 员 **依 旧** 腐 败 。

Some of the officials among them are **still** corrupt.

878 依据

yī jù

Noun: basis

nǐ de yán lùn yǒu shì shí **yī jù** ma
你 的 言 论 有 事 实 **依 据** 吗 ？

Do your statements have a factual **basis**?

879 依照

yī zhào

Preposition: according to

yī zhào jiǎn chá yuàn de zhèng jù ， tā táo bu liǎo
依 照 检 察 院 的 证 据 ， 他 逃 不 了 。

According to the prosecutor's office's evidence, he cannot escape.

880 一辈子　　yí bèi zi　　**Noun:** lifetime

kàn lái ， tā děi yí bèi zi zhù zài jiān yù
看来，他得一辈子住在监狱。
It seems that he will have to live in prison for a **lifetime**.

881 一带　　yí dài　　**Noun:** area; region

dōng nán yà yí dài huì shuō huá yǔ de rén hěn duō
东南亚一带会说华语的人很多。
Many people can speak Chinese in the Southeast Asia **region**.

882 一旦　　yí dàn　　**Adverb:** once; in case

zhàn zhēng yí dàn bào fā ， jiù hěn nán kòng zhì
战争一旦爆发，就很难控制。
Once a war breaks out, it is difficult to control.

883 一句话　　yí jù huà　　**Phrase:** in a word; in short; one sentence

jiù yí jù huà ， nǐ dào dǐ yuàn bù yuàn yì
就一句话，你到底愿不愿意？
In short, are you really willing or not?

884 一路　　yí lù　　**Adverb:** all the way; take the same route

nǐ yí lù dōu wèn wǒ zhè gè ， wǒ shòu gòu le
你一路都问我这个，我受够了！
You keep asking me this **all the way**; I've had enough!

885 一下　　yí xià　　**Noun:** a bit; a little while

wǒ yào kǎo lǜ yí xià ， bù néng lì kè dá fù nǐ
我要考虑一下，不能立刻答复你。
I have to consider **a bit** and can't answer you right away.

886 一下子　yí xià zi

Noun: all of a sudden; all at once; for a while

tā jū rán yí xià zi yòu gǎi biàn zhǔ yì le
他 居 然 一 下 子 又 改 变 主 意 了 。
He actually changed his mind **all at once** again.

887 一向　yí xiàng

Adverb: always

tā yí xiàng bù shǒu xìn wǒ yì diǎn yě bù qí guài
他 一 向 不 守 信 ， 我 一 点 也 不 奇 怪 。
He **always** doesn't keep his word, I'm not surprised at all.

888 乙　yǐ

Noun: second (traditional rank)

qǐng àn zhào jiǎ yǐ bǐng dīng de shùn xù pái liè
请 按 照 甲 乙 丙 丁 的 顺 序 排 列 。
Please arrange according to the order of first, **second**, third and fourth.

889 以便　yǐ biàn

Conjunction: so that

kuài diǎn pái liàn yǐ biàn lǐng dǎo lái jiǎn chá
快 点 排 练 ， 以 便 领 导 来 检 查 。
Rehearse quickly **so that** the leader can come to check.

890 以往　yǐ wǎng

Noun: in the past

tā yǐ wǎng nà me lǎn sàn jīn tiān zěn me qín kuài le
他 以 往 那 么 懒 散 ， 今 天 怎 么 勤 快 了 ？
He was so lazy **in the past**, why is he diligent today?

891 一口气　yì kǒu qì

Noun: one breath; in one breath

hā ha wǒ gāng gāng yì kǒu qì yóu le shí mǐ
哈 哈 ！ 我 刚 刚 一 口 气 游 了 十 米 。
Haha! I just swam ten meters **in one breath**.

892 一身　　yì shēn　　**Noun:** whole body; all over the body

suī rán yì shēn shī dàn wǒ wèi zì jǐ jiāo ào
虽然一身湿，但我为自己骄傲。
Even though my **whole body** is wet, I'm proud of myself.

893 意识　　yì shí　　**Noun:** consciousness

tā zhòng shǔ hūn dǎo hòu shī qù le yì shí
他中暑昏倒后失去了意识。
He lost **consciousness** after collapsing from heat stroke.

894 意味着　　yì wèi zhe　　**Verb:** to mean; to signify

zhè yì wèi zhe tā bù zhī dào hòu lái fā shēng de shì jiàn
这意味着他不知道后来发生的事件。
This **means** that he was unaware of subsequent events.

895 意志　　yì zhì　　**Noun:** willpower; determination

chéng gōng de rén dōu shì yì zhì jiān dìng de rén
成功的人都是意志坚定的人。
Successful people are those with a firm **willpower**.

896 因而　　yīn ér　　**Conjunction:** thus; as a result

tā men bú pà kùn nán yīn ér néng shí xiàn mù biāo
他们不怕困难，因而能实现目标。
They are not afraid of difficulties, **thus** can achieve goals.

897 饮料　　yǐn liào　　**Noun:** drinks; beverage

wǒ mā ràng wǒ shǎo hē tàn suān yǐn liào
我妈让我少喝碳酸饮料。
My mother asked me to drink less carbonated **drinks**.

170

398 饮食 yǐn shí **Noun:** diet; food and drinks

tā shuō bǎo chí jiàn kāng de yǐn shí hěn zhòng yào
她 说 保 持 健 康 的 **饮 食** 很 重 要 。
She said it's important to maintain a healthy **diet**.

399 印刷 yìn shuā **Verb:** to print (industrial)

chū bǎn shè kě yǐ zuò hēi bái hé cǎi sè yìn shuā
出 版 社 可 以 做 黑 白 和 彩 色 **印 刷** 。
The publishing house can do black and white as well as color **printing**.

400a 应 yīng **Verb:** should; ought to

jiàng dī chéng běn yīng shì shǒu yào rèn wù duì ma
降 低 成 本 **应** 是 首 要 任 务 , 对 吗 ?
Reducing costs **should** be a priority, right?

400b 应 yìng **Verb:** to answer; to respond

nǐ rú guǒ bù yìng jiù dài biǎo fǎn duì
你 如 果 不 **应** , 就 代 表 反 对 。
If you don't **respond**, it means you are against it.

401 硬 yìng **Adjective:** hard

tā pí qì yìng bié guǎn tā
他 脾 气 **硬** , 别 管 他 !
He has a **hard** temper, leave him alone!

402 硬件 yìng jiàn **Noun:** hardware

wǒ men yòng wú rén pèi sòng chē yùn shū zhè xiē yìng jiàn
我 们 用 无 人 配 送 车 运 输 这 些 **硬 件** 。
We transport these **hardware** in autonomous delivery vehicles.

903 拥抱 yōng bào

Verb: to hug; to embrace
Noun: hug

Verb
dāng shí wǒ men dà gài yōng bào le wǔ fēn zhōng
当 时 我 们 大 概 **拥 抱** 了 五 分 钟。
At that time, we probably **hugged** for 5 minutes.

Noun
nà shì yí gè hěn wēn nuǎn de yōng bào
那 是 一 个 很 温 暖 的 **拥 抱**。
That was a very warm **hug**.

904 拥有 yōng yǒu

Verb: to have; to own

yǒu de rén yōng yǒu jù dà de cái fù hé quán lì
有 的 人 **拥 有** 巨 大 的 财 富 和 权 力。
Some people **have** great wealth and power.

905 用不着 yòng bu zháo

Phrase: no need; have no use

tā men zhǐ xiǎng lè yòng bu zháo dān xīn shēng huó
他 们 只 享 乐，**用 不 着** 担 心 生 活。
They only have fun, **no need** to worry about life.

906 用户 yòng hù

Noun: user

guó jì dǒu yīn yòng hù zhì shǎo yǒu jǐ shí yì
国 际 抖 音 **用 户** 至 少 有 几 十 亿。
There are at least several billion international TikTok **users**.

907 用来 yòng lái

Verb: to use to

tài yáng huā bù jǐn měi ér qiě kě yǐ yòng lái chī
太 阳 花 不 仅 美，而 且 可 以 **用 来** 吃。
Sunflowers are not only beautiful, they can also **be used to** eat.

908 用于   yòng yú   **Verb:** to use for/in/on

tā kě yòng yú yī yào   yě kě yòng yú měi shí
它 可 **用 于** 医 药 ， 也 可 **用 于** 美 食 。
It can be **used in** medicine, as well as **used in** cuisine.

---

909 优惠   yōu huì   **Noun:** discount
Adjective: favorable; preferential

Noun
jīn tiān shì shuāng shí yī   shāng diàn yǒu hěn duō yōu huì
今 天 是 双 十 一 ， 商 店 有 很 多 **优 惠** 。
Today is Double 11 Day, there are many **discounts** in stores.

Adj.
zhè gè zhì néng shǒu jī de jià gé hěn yōu huì
这 个 智 能 手 机 的 价 格 很 **优 惠** 。
The price of this smartphone is **favorable**.

---

910 优先   yōu xiān   **Verb:** to prioritize; to give priority

zhè xiē shì xū yào yōu xiān wán chéng de rèn wù
这 些 是 需 要 **优 先** 完 成 的 任 务 。
These are the tasks that need to be **prioritized** (to finish).

---

911 幽默   yōu mò   **Adjective:** humorous
Noun: humor

Adj.
wǒ lǎo gōng jiù xiàng zhǐ hóu zi   fēi cháng yōu mò
我 老 公 就 像 只 猴 子 ， 非 常 **幽 默** 。
My husband is like a monkey, very **humorous**.

Noun
tā de yōu mò hé zhì huì dōu shì xìng gé liàng diǎn
他 的 **幽 默** 和 智 慧 都 是 性 格 亮 点 。
His **humor** and wisdom are both character highlights.

---

912 尤其   yóu qí   **Adverb:** especially

tā hěn hǎo wán   jiǎng de xiào huà yóu qí gǎo xiào
他 很 好 玩 ， 讲 的 笑 话 **尤 其** 搞 笑 。
He is very fun and his jokes are **especially** funny.

913 由此 yóu cǐ

Conjunction: thus; therefore

hé tong yǐn cáng le wèn tí yóu cǐ yǐn qǐ le zhēng zhí
合同隐藏了问题，**由此**引起了争执。
The contract has hidden issues, **thus** triggers disputes.

914 犹豫 yóu yù

Verb: to hesitate
Noun: hesitation

Verb
bú yào yóu yù yào xiāng xìn nǐ de pàn duàn
不要**犹豫**，要相信你的判断！
Don't **hesitate**, trust your judgment!

Noun
yóu yù shì nǐ zuì dà de xìng gé ruò diǎn
犹豫是你最大的性格弱点。
Hesitation is your greatest character weakness.

915 游泳池 yóu yǒng chí

Noun: swimming pool

wǒ xiǎng yōng yǒu yí tào dài yóu yǒng chí de bié shù
我想拥有一套带**游泳池**的别墅。
I want to own a villa with a **swimming pool**.

916 友谊 yǒu yì

Noun: friendship

yǒu yì bǐ ài qíng gèng chí jiǔ yě gèng kě kào
友谊比爱情更持久，也更可靠。
Friendship is more durable and reliable than romantic love.

917 有毒 yǒu dú

Adjective: poisonous; venomous

zhè zhǒng yě mó gū yǒu dú bù néng chī
这种野蘑菇**有毒**，不能吃。
This wild mushroom is **poisonous** and cannot be eaten.

918 有害　　yǒu hài　　**Adjective:** harmful; pernicious

rú guǒ chī le, kěn dìng duì nǐ de jiàn kāng yǒu hài
如果吃了，肯定对你的健康有害。
If you eat it, it will definitely be **harmful** to your health.

919 有力　　yǒu lì　　**Adjective:** energetic; powerful; vigorous

wǒ gǎn jué zài shàng wǔ yǒu lì, xià wǔ wú lì
我感觉在上午有力，下午无力。
I feel **energetic** in the morning and lethargic (without energy) in the afternoon.

920 有利于　　yǒu lì yú　　**Verb:** to favor; to benefit

duō chī shū cài yǒu lì yú zēng qiáng miǎn yì lì
多吃蔬菜有利于增强免疫力。
Eating more vegetables will **benefit** enhancing immunity.

921 有着　　yǒu zhe　　**Verb:** to have; to possess

tè bié shì hú luó bo, yǒu zhe fēng fù de yíng yǎng
特别是胡萝卜，有着丰富的营养。
Carrots, in particular, **possess** rich nutrients.

922 羽毛球　　yǔ máo qiú　　**Noun:** badminton

tā yíng guò jiǎng bēi, shì dǎ yǔ máo qiú de gāo shǒu
他赢过奖杯，是打羽毛球的高手。
He has won trophies and is a master at playing **badminton**.

923 羽绒服　　yǔ róng fú　　**Noun:** down jacket

zhè jiàn yǔ róng fú zhì liàng hǎo, chuān zhe yě shū fu
这件羽绒服质量好，穿着也舒服。
This **down jacket** is of good quality and comfortable to wear.

924 雨水　yǔ shuǐ

Noun: rainwater; rainfall

ér qiě tā fáng shuǐ　bú yì bèi yǔ shuǐ nòng shī
而且它防水，不易被雨水弄湿。
And it's waterproof and won't get wet easily from **rainwater**.

925 预备　yù bèi

Verb: to prepare; to get ready

wǒ zài zhuān xīn yù bèi yí gè gōng zuò miàn shì
我在专心预备一个工作面试。
I'm concentrating on **preparing** for a job interview.

926 预期　yù qī

Verb: to expect; to anticipate
Noun: expectation

Verb
wǒ yù qī néng zài liǎng zhōu nèi wán chéng miàn shì guò chéng
我预期能在两周内完成面试过程。
I **expect** to be through the interview process within 2 weeks.

Noun
wǒ dān xīn zì jǐ de biǎo xiàn méi yǒu yù qī de hǎo
我担心自己的表现没有预期的好。
I worry that my performance is not as good as **expectations**.

927 元旦　yuán dàn

New Year's Day

zhè bù hǎo lái wù diàn yǐng huì zài yuán dàn shàng yìng
这部好莱坞电影会在元旦上映。
This Hollywood movie will be released on **New Year's Day**.

928 园林　yuán lín

Noun: landscape garden

nǐ cān guān guò běi jīng jǐng shān gōng yuán de yuán lín ma
你参观过北京景山公园的园林吗？
Have you visited the **gardens** of Jingshan Park in Beijing?

929 原理 yuán lǐ **Noun:** principle (theory)

那 里 的 亭 子 体 现 了 中 式 建 筑 原 理 。
nà lǐ de tíng zi tǐ xiàn le zhōng shì jiàn zhù yuán lǐ
The pavilion there embodies the **principles** of Chinese architecture.

930 原始 yuán shǐ **Adjective:** primitive; firsthand

李 教 授 热 衷 于 研 究 原 始 社 会 。
lǐ jiào shòu rè zhōng yú yán jiū yuán shǐ shè huì
Professor Li is passionate about studying **primitive** societies.

931 原先 yuán xiān **Adverb:** at first; originally

他 原 先 没 有 进 展 ， 但 是 现 在 有 了 。
tā yuán xiān méi yǒu jìn zhǎn dàn shì xiàn zài yǒu le
He had no progress **at first**, but now he has.

932 原有 yuán yǒu **Adjective:** original (once existed)

这 是 这 座 教 堂 原 有 的 设 计 模 型 。
zhè shì zhè zuò jiào táng yuán yǒu de shè jì mó xíng
This is the **original** design model of this church.

933 远处 yuǎn chù **Noun:** in the distance; far away

远 处 的 风 景 比 近 处 的 更 美 。
yuǎn chù de fēng jǐng bǐ jìn chù de gèng měi
The scenery **in the distance** is more beautiful than nearby.

934 怨 yuàn **Verb:** to blame; to complain

如 果 你 懒 得 跟 我 们 去 ， 就 别 怨 我 。
rú guǒ nǐ lǎn de gēn wǒ men qù jiù bié yuàn wǒ
If you're too lazy to come with us, then don't **blame** me.

935 愿   yuàn   **Verb:** to be willing; to hope

^{tā} ^{bú} ^{yuàn} ^{biàn} ^{chéng} ^{rèn} ^{hé} ^{rén} ^{de} ^{fù} ^{dān}
她 不 愿 变 成 任 何 人 的 负 担 。
She is not **willing** to be a burden to anyone.

936 约束   yuē shù   **Verb:** to bind; to restrain
Noun: restraint

Verb
^{rú} ^{guǒ} ^{nǐ} ^{zhēn} ^{xīn} ^{ài} ^{tā} ^{jiù} ^{bú} ^{yào} ^{yuē} ^{shù} ^{tā}
如 果 你 真 心 爱 她 ， 就 不 要 约 束 她 。
If you truly love her, don't **restrain** her.

Noun
^{yuē} ^{shù} ^{zhǐ} ^{huì} ^{zào} ^{chéng} ^{shāng} ^{hài} ^{hé} ^{yuàn} ^{hèn}
约 束 只 会 造 成 伤 害 和 怨 恨 。
Restraint only creates hurt and resentment.

937 月饼   yuè bǐng   **Noun:** mooncake

^{wǒ} ^{zuì} ^{ài} ^{chī} ^{hóng} ^{dòu} ^{shā} ^{yuè} ^{bǐng} ^{nǐ} ^{ne}
我 最 爱 吃 红 豆 沙 **月 饼** ， 你 呢 ？
I love eating red bean paste **mooncakes** the most, what about you?

938 月球   yuè qiú   **Noun:** the Moon (scientific term)

^{háng} ^{tiān} ^{yuán} ^{men} ^{yòu} ^{qù} ^{yuè} ^{qiú} ^{tàn} ^{xiǎn} ^{le}
航 天 员 们 又 去 **月 球** 探 险 了 ！
The astronauts went to explore **the Moon** again!

939 阅览室   yuè lǎn shì   **Noun:** reading room

^{wǒ} ^{jīn} ^{zǎo} ^{zài} ^{yuè} ^{lǎn} ^{shì} ^{dāi} ^{le} ^{sān} ^{gè} ^{bàn} ^{xiǎo} ^{shí}
我 今 早 在 **阅 览 室** 呆 了 三 个 半 小 时 。
I spent 3 and a half hours in the **reading room** this morning.

940 运   yùn   **Verb:** to transport; to carry

shéi fù zé cóng shēn zhèn yùn huò dào guǎng zhōu
谁 负 责 从 深 圳 **运** 货 到 广 州 ？
Who's responsible for **transporting** goods from Shenzhen to Guangzhou?

941 运行   yùn xíng   **Verb:** to run/work (machine or systems)

tīng shuō wú rén jià shǐ de chū zū chē yùn xíng de hěn hǎo
听 说 无 人 驾 驶 的 出 租 车 **运 行** 得 很 好 。
I heard driverless taxis are **working** very well.

942 灾   zāi   **Noun:** disaster; calamity (use with other words)

zhè lǐ de shuǐ zāi fā shēng lǜ dī yú píng jūn shuǐ píng
这 里 的 **水 灾** 发 生 率 低 于 平 均 水 平 。
The rate of **flooding** here is lower than the average level.

943 灾害   zāi hài   **Noun:** disaster (natural)

qì hòu bù hǎo róng yì dǎo zhì zì rán zāi hài
气 候 不 好 容 易 导 致 自 然 **灾 害** 。
Bad climate can easily lead to natural **disasters**.

944 灾难   zāi nàn   **Noun:** disaster (natural or man-made)

zhè chǎng zhàn zhēng shì shàng gè shì jì zuì dà de zhèng
这 场 战 争 是 上 个 世 纪 最 大 的 政
zhì zāi nàn
治 **灾 难** 。
This war was the greatest political **disaster** of the past century.

945 灾区   zāi qū   **Noun:** disaster area

zāi qū de jīng jì yě shòu dào le jù dà de yǐng xiǎng
灾区 的 经 济 也 受 到 了 巨 大 的 影 响 。
The economy of the **disaster area** was also greatly affected.

946 再次   zài cì   **Adverb:** once more; once again

rú guǒ zāi nàn zài cì lái lín hòu guǒ shì huǐ miè xìng de
如 果 灾 难 **再次** 来 临 ， 后 果 是 毁 灭 性 的 。
If disaster strikes **once again**, the consequences will be devastating.

947 再也   zài yě   **Adverb:** anymore; no longer

yīn cǐ dà jiā zài yě bù xiǎng juǎn rù zhàn zhēng
因 此 ， 大 家 **再也** 不 想 卷 入 战 争 。
Therefore, no one wants to be involved in a war **anymore**.

948 在场   zài chǎng   **Verb:** to be present; be on the scene

qǐng zài chǎng de gè wèi suí biàn fā biǎo yì jiàn
请 **在场** 的 各 位 随 便 发 表 意 见 。
Everyone **present** please feel free to express your opinions.

949 在内   zài nèi   **Verb:** to include

wǒ zài nèi yí gòng yǒu bā gè lán qiú duì yuán
我 **在内** ， 一 共 有 八 个 篮 球 队 员 。
Including me, there are 8 basketball players in total.

950 暂时　zàn shí

Adjective: temporary
Noun: for the time being

Adj.
lì yì shì zàn shí de　gǎn qíng shì cháng yuǎn de
利益是**暂时**的，感情是长远的。
Benefits are **temporary**, relationships are long-lasting.

Noun
wǒ men tài máng　zàn shí bù dǎ suàn jié hūn
我们太忙，**暂时**不打算结婚。
We're too busy and don't plan to get married **for the time being**.

951 暂停　zàn tíng

Verb: to pause;
to suspend

wǒ jiàn yì zàn tíng bǐ sài　xiān jiě jué chōng tū
我建议**暂停**比赛，先解决冲突。
I suggest **pausing** the match and resolving the conflict first.

952 糟(糕)　zāo (gāo)

Adjective: bad;
messy; terrible

zāo gāo　liǎng fāng de qiú mí zài dǎ jià
糟糕！两方的球迷在打架。
Terrible! Football fans from both sides are fighting.

953 早期　zǎo qī

Noun: early stage;
early phase

wǒ shōu jí le zhè gè huà jiā de yì xiē zǎo qī zuò pǐn
我收集了这个画家的一些**早期**作品。
I have collected some of this painter's **early** (**stage**) works.

954 增　zēng

Verb: to grow;
to add; to increase

wǒ duì tā de yǎng mù yǒu zēng wú jiǎn
我对他的仰慕有**增**无减。
My admiration for him only **grows**, never decreases.

955 增产   zēng chǎn   **Verb:** to increase production

_{wèi le bǎo zhèng zhì liàng   zēng chǎn yīng gāi shèn zhòng}
为 了 保 证 质 量 ， **增 产** 应 该 慎 重 。
To ensure quality, you should **increase production** cautiously.

956 增大   zēng dà   **Verb:** to enlarge; to magnify

_{gōng sī jì huà zēng dà jiàn zhù gōng chéng de fàn wéi}
公 司 计 划 **增 大** 建 筑 工 程 的 范 围 。
The company plans **to enlarge** the scope of construction work.

957 增多   zēng duō   **Verb:** to increase (grow in number)

_{rú guǒ yù suàn zēng duō shéi néng tí gōng zī jīn}
如 果 预 算 **增 多** ， 谁 能 提 供 资 金 ？
If the budget **increases**, who can provide the funds?

958 增强   zēng qiáng   **Verb:** to enhance; to strengthen

_{tóu zī zhě men xī wàng zēng qiáng gōng sī de jìng zhēng lì}
投 资 者 们 希 望 **增 强** 公 司 的 竞 争 力 。
Investors hope **to enhance** the company's competitiveness.

959 赠(送)   zèng (sòng)   **Verb:** to gift

_{zhè fú huà shàng xiě zhe   zèng hǎo yǒu míng míng}
这 幅 画 上 写 着 ： **赠** 好 友 明 明 。
This painting reads: **Gift** to Good Friend MingMing.

960 摘   zhāi   **Verb:** to pick (plants)

_{tā men yuē wǒ qù xiāng xià zhāi cǎo méi}
他 们 约 我 去 乡 下 **摘** 草 莓 。
They invited me to go to the countryside **to pick** strawberries.

961 展览　zhǎn lǎn　**Noun:** exhibition

tóng shì men zài wèi zhè cì zhǎn lǎn xuān chuán
同 事 们 在 为 这 次 **展 览** 宣 传 。
Colleagues are promoting this **exhibition**.

962 展示　zhǎn shì　**Verb:** to showcase; to exhibit

wǒ men huì zhǎn shì gōng sī de zuì xīn chǎn pǐn
我 们 会 **展 示** 公 司 的 最 新 产 品 。
We will **showcase** the company's latest products.

963 展现　zhǎn xiàn　**Verb:** to demonstrate

chǎn pǐn de gōng néng yě huì zài huì yì shàng zhǎn xiàn
产 品 的 功 能 也 会 在 会 议 上 **展 现** 。
The functionality of the product will also be **demonstrated** at the meeting.

964 占领　zhàn lǐng　**Verb:** to occupy (territory)

kǒng bù fēn zǐ de jūn duì gāng gāng zhàn lǐng le yí zuò chéng
恐 怖 分 子 的 军 队 刚 刚 **占 领** 了 一 座 城 。
The terrorist army has just **occupied** a city.

965 占有　zhàn yǒu　**Verb:** to hold; to possess

tā men méi yǒu dào yì bú zhàn yǒu zhèng zhì yōu shì
他 们 没 有 道 义 , 不 **占 有** 政 治 优 势 。
They lack morality and do not **hold** a political advantage.

966 涨　zhǎng　**Verb:** to rise

cháo shuǐ zài zhǎng bú yào zài zhè shí yóu yǒng
潮 水 在 **涨** , 不 要 在 这 时 游 泳 。
The tide is **rising**, do not swim at this time.

967 涨价   zhǎng jià   **Verb: to rise in price**

促销结束后，商品会涨价。
cù xiāo jié shù hòu, shāng pǐn huì zhǎng jià

After the promotion ends, the product's **price** will **rise**.

968 掌握   zhǎng wò   **Verb: to master**

掌握有效的促销策略是关键。
zhǎng wò yǒu xiào de cù xiāo cè lüè shì guān jiàn

Mastering effective promotional strategies is key.

969 招生   zhāo shēng   **Verb: to enroll students**

学校在忙招生，我必须加班。
xué xiào zài máng zhāo shēng, wǒ bì xū jiā bān

The school's busy **enrolling students**; I have to work overtime.

970 招手   zhāo shǒu   **Verb: to wave; to beckon**

我看到一个性感美女向他招手。
wǒ kàn dào yí gè xìng gǎn měi nǚ xiàng tā zhāo shǒu

I saw a sexy beauty **waving** at him.

971 珍贵   zhēn guì   **Adjective: precious**

我们有过一段快乐而珍贵的时光。
wǒ men yǒu guò yí duàn kuài lè ér zhēn guì de shí guāng

We had a happy and **precious** time.

972 珍惜   zhēn xī   **Verb: to cherish**

我很珍惜我们的友谊和那些回忆。
wǒ hěn zhēn xī wǒ men de yǒu yì hé nà xiē huí yì

I **cherish** our friendship and those memories.

973 珍珠   zhēn zhū   **Noun:** pearl

wǒ yì zhí zhēn cáng zhe tā sòng wǒ de zhēn zhū xiàng liàn
我 一 直 珍 藏 着 他 送 我 的 **珍 珠** 项 链 。
I've always treasured the **pearl** necklace he gave me.

974 真诚   zhēn chéng   **Adjective:** sincere; genuine
                                           Noun: sincerity; genuineness

Adj.   zhēn chéng de gǎn qíng shì wú jià de
真 诚 的 感 情 是 无 价 的 。
Sincere relationships are priceless.

Noun   wǒ men dōu bèi tā de zhēn chéng gǎn dòng le
我 们 都 被 他 的 **真 诚** 感 动 了 。
We were all moved by his **sincerity**.

975 真理   zhēn lǐ   **Noun:** truth (conceptually)

shēng lǎo bìng sǐ shì bú biàn de zhēn lǐ
生 老 病 死 是 不 变 的 **真 理** 。
Birth, aging, sickness and death are unchanging **truths**.

976 真相   zhēn xiàng   **Noun:** truth (factually)

shòu hài zhě zài fǎ tíng shàng shuō chū le zhēn xiàng
受 害 者 在 法 庭 上 说 出 了 **真 相** 。
The victim told the **truth** in court.

977 诊断   zhěn duàn   **Verb:** to diagnose
                                           Noun: diagnosis

Verb   yī shēng zài gěi tā zhěn duàn xīn zàng
医 生 在 给 他 **诊 断** 心 脏 。
The doctor is **diagnosing** his heart.

Noun   gēn jù zhěn duàn tā yǒu xīn zàng bìng hé táng niào bìng
根 据 **诊 断** ， 他 有 心 脏 病 和 糖 尿 病 。
According to the **diagnosis**, he had heart disease and diabetes.

978 振动　　zhèn dòng　　**Verb:** to vibrate

rú guǒ nǐ bù xiǎng shǒu jī zhèn dòng， jiù jìng yīn
如果你不想手机**振动**，就静音。
If you don't want your phone **to vibrate**, mute it.

979 震惊　　zhèn jīng　　**Adjective:** shocked; shocking

dà jiā duì qián shǒu xiàng zuò láo hěn zhèn jīng
大家对前首相坐牢很**震惊**。
Everyone is **shocked** that the former prime minister is in jail.

980 争议　　zhēng yì　　**Noun:** dispute; controversy

qí shí tā yì zhí shì gè yǒu zhēng yì de lǐng dǎo
其实他一直是个有**争议**的领导。
In fact, he has always been a leader of **controversy**.

981 正版　　zhèng bǎn　　**Noun:** legal copy; official edition

tā mǎi de shū shì dào bǎn， nǐ de cái shì zhèng bǎn
他买的书是盗版，你的才是**正版**。
The book he bought is a pirated edition, only yours is the **official edition**.

982 正规　　zhèng guī　　**Adjective:** regular; standard

dào bǎn de fā xíng tú jìng bú zhèng guī
盗版的发行途径不**正规**。
The distribution channels of pirated copies are ir**regular**.

983 正如　　zhèng rú　　**Adverb:** just as; exactly as

zhèng rú nǐ shuō， zhè jiǎn zhí shì qīn quán xíng wéi
正如你说，这简直是侵权行为。
Just as you said, this is simply an act of infringement.

984 正义　　zhèng yì　　**Noun:** justice

hàn wèi zhèng yì shì lì fǎ de mù dì
捍 卫 **正 义** 是 立 法 的 目 的 。
Defending **justice** is the purpose of legislation.

985 证实　　zhèng shí　　**Verb:** to confirm (truth)

yí dàn bèi zhèng shí tā men bì xū péi cháng nǐ de sǔn shī
一 旦 被 **证 实** ，他 们 必 须 赔 偿 你 的 损 失 。
Once **confirmed**, they must compensate you for your losses.

986 证书　　zhèng shū　　**Noun:** certificate

wǒ shì tā men jié hūn zhèng shū shàng de jiàn zhèng rén
我 是 他 们 结 婚 **证 书** 上 的 见 证 人 。
I am a witness on their marriage **certificate**.

987 挣　　zhèng　　**Verb:** to earn; to struggle to get free (use with other words)

tā lǎo pó měi gè yuè cái zhèng yì qiān měi yuán
他 老 婆 每 个 月 才 **挣** 一 千 美 元 。
His wife only **earns** a thousand dollars a month.

xìng kuī tā dāng shí zhèng tuō le shéng suǒ táo pǎo le
幸 亏 他 当 时 **挣 脱** 了 绳 索 ， 逃 跑 了 。
Luckily, at that time, he **broke free** from the rope and run away.

988 挣钱　　zhèng qián　　**Verb:** to make/earn money

tā nǔ lì zhèng qián tā què nǔ lì huā qián
她 努 力 **挣 钱** ， 他 却 努 力 花 钱 。
She worked hard **to make money**, but he worked hard to spend it.

989 之内   zhī nèi   **Preposition:** in; within

zài sān nián zhī nèi tā men kěn dìng huì pò chǎn
在 三 年 **之 内** 他 们 肯 定 会 破 产 。
Within 3 years they will certainly be bankrupt.

990 之外   zhī wài   **Preposition:** outside; except

zhè jué duì bú huì shì yù liào zhī wài de shì
这 绝 对 不 会 是 预 料 **之 外** 的 事 。
This will definitely not be something **outside** of expectations.

991 之下   zhī xià   **Preposition:** under

zài tā de lǐng dǎo zhī xià ， gōng sī shàng shì le
在 他 的 领 导 **之 下** ， 公 司 上 市 了 。
Under his leadership, the company went public.

992 之中   zhī zhōng   **Preposition:** among; in the midst of

tā yě zài dǒng shì huì de chéng yuán zhī zhōng
他 也 在 董 事 会 的 成 员 **之 中** 。
He is also **among** the members of the board of directors.

993 支出   zhī chū   **Verb:** to expend; to pay out
Noun: expenses; outlay

Verb
gōng sī yí gòng xiàng tā men zhī chū le bā shí wǔ wàn yuán
公 司 一 共 向 他 们 **支 出** 了 八 十 五 万 元 。
The company **paid** them 850,000 yuan in total.

Noun
zhè shì wǒ zhěng lǐ de zhī chū hé shōu rù bào gào
这 是 我 整 理 的 **支 出** 和 收 入 报 告 。
Here is the **expense** and income report I put together.

994 支配　　　　zhī pèi　　　**Verb:** to allocate; to govern
Noun: allocation

Verb
zǒng jiān fù zé zhī pèi bù mén de rèn wù
总 监 负 责 **支 配** 部 门 的 任 务 。
The director is in charge of **allocating** tasks of the department.

Noun
tā huì jǐn liàng shí xiàn gōng píng zhī pèi
他 会 尽 量 实 现 公 平 **支 配** 。
He will try to achieve fair **allocation**.

995 执行　　　　zhí xíng　　　**Verb:** to execute; to implement
Noun: execution

Verb
wǒ yào xiǎng bàn fǎ zhí xíng zhè gè fāng àn
我 要 想 办 法 **执 行** 这 个 方 案 。
I want to find a way to **implement** this scheme.

Noun
zhè shì duì wǒ zhí xíng néng lì de yí gè tiǎo zhàn
这 是 对 我 **执 行** 能 力 的 一 个 挑 战 。
This is a challenge to my **execution** ability.

996 直线　　　　zhí xiàn　　　**Noun:** straight line

jīng jì fā zhǎn de xiàn shì qū xiàn bú shì zhí xiàn
经 济 发 展 的 线 是 曲 线 ， 不 是 **直 线** 。
The line of economic development is a curve, not a **straight line**.

997 值班　　　　zhí bān　　　**Verb:** to be on duty

wǒ jīn wǎn yào zhí bān bù néng hé nǐ men chī wǎn fàn
我 今 晚 要 **值 班** ， 不 能 和 你 们 吃 晚 饭 。
I have **to be on duty** tonight and can't have dinner with you.

998 职能　　　　zhí néng　　　**Noun:** function (job role)

wěi yuán huì de zhǔ yào zhí néng shì jiān dū
委 员 会 的 主 要 **职 能** 是 监 督 。
The main **function** of the committee is supervision.

999 职位   zhí wèi   **Noun:** position (job)

zhè gè **zhí wèi** fù zé píng gū yuán gōng biǎo xiàn
这 个 **职 位** 负 责 评 估 员 工 表 现 。

This **position** bears responsibility for evaluating employee performance.

1000 职务   zhí wù   **Noun:** duty (work)

zhè gè **zhí wù** zhòng dà ér fù zá
这 个 **职 务** 重 大 而 复 杂 。

This **duty** is important and complex.

1001 只不过   zhǐ bú guò   **Adverb:** just; merely

tā qián qī **zhǐ bú guò** shì tā rén shēng de guò kè
他 前 妻 **只 不 过** 是 他 人 生 的 过 客 。

His ex-wife was **just** a passer-by in his life.

1002 只见   zhǐ jiàn   **Verb:** to only see

bù yào **zhǐ jiàn** guò qù, tā zǎo jiù xiàng qián zǒu le
不 要 **只 见** 过 去 ， 他 早 就 向 前 走 了 。

Don't **only see** the past, he has moved forward a long time ago.

1003 指标   zhǐ biāo   **Noun:** indicator; target; index

wǒ yòng jīng jì **zhǐ biāo** píng gū shì chǎng zǒu shì
我 用 经 济 **指 标** 评 估 市 场 走 势 。

I use economic **indicators** to evaluate market trends.

1004 指甲   zhǐ jia   **Noun:** nail

tā gāng gāng qù měi jiǎ diàn xiū **zhǐ jia** le
她 刚 刚 去 美 甲 店 修 **指 甲** 了 。

She just went to the nail salon to get her **nails** done.

1005 指示   zhǐ shì

Verb: to instruct
Noun: instruction

Verb
经 理 说 要 **指 示** 我 完 成 项 目 。
jīng lǐ shuō yào zhǐ shì wǒ wán chéng xiàng mù
The manager said he'll **instruct** me to complete the project.

Noun
我 懂 流 程 ， 不 需 要 他 的 **指 示** 。
wǒ dǒng liú chéng bù xū yào tā de zhǐ shì
I understand the process and don't need his **instructions**.

1006 指责   zhǐ zé

Verb: to accuse
Noun: accusation

Verb
我 会 自 己 承 担 责 任 ， 不 会 **指 责** 别 人 。
wǒ huì zì jǐ chéng dān zé rèn bú huì zhǐ zé bié rén
I will take responsibility for myself and will not **accuse** others.

Noun
反 正 **指 责** 和 抱 怨 都 没 用 。
fǎn zhèng zhǐ zé hé bào yuàn dōu méi yòng
Accusation and complaints are both useless anyway.

1007 至   zhì

Preposition: to; till; until

老 板 从 早 **至** 晚 都 没 离 开 过 办 公 室 。
lǎo bǎn cóng zǎo zhì wǎn dōu méi lí kāi guò bàn gōng shì
The boss never left the office from morning **to** night.

1008 制成   zhì chéng

Verb: to make into

我 把 他 送 我 的 丝 绸 **制 成** 了 围 巾 。
wǒ bǎ tā sòng wǒ de sī chóu zhì chéng le wéi jīn
I **made** the silk he gave me **into** a scarf.

1009 制约   zhì yuē

Verb: restrict (law or system); to check and balance

行 政 机 构 和 立 法 机 构 相 互 **制 约** 。
xíng zhèng jī gòu hé lì fǎ jī gòu xiāng hù zhì yuē
The executive and legislative bodies **check and balance** each other.

1010 治安   zhì ān   **Noun:** public security

wǒ de dà xué zhuān yè shì zhì ān guǎn lǐ
我 的 大 学 专 业 是 **治 安** 管 理 。
My university major was **public security** management.

1011 治理   zhì lǐ   **Verb:** to govern; to administer

duō shù zhèng kè dōu bú shàn cháng zhì lǐ guó jiā
多 数 政 客 都 不 擅 长 **治 理** 国 家 。
Most politicians are not good at **governing** a country.

1012 中断   zhōng duàn   **Verb:** to interrupt; to pause

diàn shì jù bèi guǎng gào zhōng duàn le zhēn tǎo yàn
电 视 剧 被 广 告 **中 断** 了 ， 真 讨 厌 ！
The TV series is **interrupted** by advertisements, so annoying!

1013 中秋节   zhōng qiū jié   **Noun:** Mid-Autumn Festival

zhè gè gù shì shì guān yú zhōng qiū jié de lái yuán
这 个 故 事 是 关 于 **中 秋 节** 的 来 源 。
This story is about the origin of the **Mid-Autumn Festival**.

1014 中央   zhōng yāng   **Noun:** center

tā shì zhōng yāng diàn shì tái de zhōng qiū wǎn huì jié mù
它 是 **中 央** 电 视 台 的 中 秋 晚 会 节 目 。
It is the Mid-Autumn Festival Gala program of CCTV (China **Central** Television).

1015 中药   zhōng yào   **Noun:** (traditional) Chinese medicine

zhōng yào de wèi dào tài kǔ wǒ tǎo yàn hē
中 药 的 味 道 太 苦 ， 我 讨 厌 喝 。
The taste of **Chinese medicine** is so bitter, I dislike drinking it.

1016 终点

zhōng diǎn

Noun: ending; the end

zhè liǎng biān shì sài pǎo lù xiàn de qǐ diǎn hé zhōng diǎn
这 两 边 是 赛 跑 路 线 的 起 点 和 **终 点** 。
These two sides are the start and **end** points of the race route.

1017 终身

zhōng shēn

Noun: lifelong; in one's lifetime

wǒ bù míng bái wèi hé wǒ ā yí zhōng shēn bù hūn
我 不 明 白 为 何 我 阿 姨 **终 身** 不 婚 。
I don't understand why my aunt never married all her **lifetime**.

1018 终止

zhōng zhǐ

Verb: to terminate
Noun: termination

Verb

tiān a wǒ de zhàng hào tū rán bèi zhōng zhǐ le
天 啊 ! 我 的 账 号 突 然 被 **终 止** 了 。
Oh god! My account is suddenly **terminated**.

Noun

wǒ děi mǎ shàng lián xì yín háng jiě chú zhōng zhǐ
我 得 马 上 联 系 银 行 解 除 **终 止** 。
I have to contact the bank immediately to lift the **termination**.

1019 中毒

zhòng dú

Verb: to be poisoned

tā zhòng dú le bì xū sòng qù jí zhěn shì
他 **中 毒** 了 , 必 须 送 去 急 诊 室 。
He was **poisoned**, had to be taken to the emergency room.

1020 众多

zhòng duō

Adjective: many; numerous

zhè dú shì zhòng duō dú sù lǐ zuì nán jiě de
这 毒 是 **众 多** 毒 素 里 最 难 解 的 。
This poison is the most difficult to detoxify among **many** toxins.

1021 周期   zhōu qī   **Noun:** cycle; period

这 种 植 物 的 生 长 周 期 是 三 到 四 个 月 。
zhè zhǒng zhí wù de shēng zhǎng zhōu qī shì sān dào sì gè yuè

The growth **cycle** of this type of plant is 3 to 4 months.

1022 竹子   zhú zi   **Noun:** bamboo

竹 子 不 仅 优 雅 ， 而 且 生 命 力 强 。
zhú zi bù jǐn yōu yǎ ér qiě shēng mìng lì qiáng

Bamboo is not only elegant, but also strong in vitality.

1023 主办   zhǔ bàn   **Verb:** to host

王 总 负 责 主 办 今 年 的 圣 诞 晚 会 。
wáng zǒng fù zé zhǔ bàn jīn nián de shèng dàn wǎn huì

Boss Wang is responsible for **hosting** this year's Christmas party.

1024 主导   zhǔ dǎo   **Adjective:** leading; dominating

他 在 人 事 部 门 占 主 导 地 位 。
tā zài rén shì bù mén zhàn zhǔ dǎo dì wèi

He holds a **leading** position in the HR department.

1025 主观   zhǔ guān   **Adjective:** subjective

他 的 想 法 太 主 观 ， 不 够 客 观 。
tā de xiǎng fǎ tài zhǔ guān bù gòu kè guān

His ideas are too **subjective**, not objective enough.

1026 主管   zhǔ guǎn   **Noun:** supervisor; executive director

这 个 主 管 刚 刚 被 上 级 炒 了 。
zhè gè zhǔ guǎn gāng gāng bèi shàng jí chǎo le

This **director** has just been fired by his superior.

1027 主体　　　　　zhǔ tǐ　　　**Noun:** main body; main part

tā céng shuō yuán gōng shì gōng sī de zhǔ tǐ
他 曾 说 员 工 是 公 司 的 **主 体**。
He once said that employees are the **main body** of the company.

1028 助理　　　　　zhù lǐ　　　**Noun:** assistant (job role)

tīng shuō tā zuì zhōng chéng de zhù lǐ yě cí zhí le
听 说 他 最 忠 诚 的 **助 理** 也 辞 职 了。
I heard his most loyal **assistant** also resigned.

1029 助手　　　　　zhù shǒu　　　**Noun:** assistant (general)

wǒ mā zài zuò dàn gāo xū yào yí gè zhù shǒu
我 妈 在 做 蛋 糕， 需 要 一 个 **助 手**。
My mother is making cakes and needs an **assistant**.

1030 注册　　　　　zhù cè　　　**Verb:** to register
　　　　　　　　　　　　　　　　　　Noun: registration

Verb
qí shí zhù cè gōng sī de chéng xù bú fù zá
其 实， **注 册** 公 司 的 程 序 不 复 杂。
In fact, the procedure for **registering** a company is not complex.

Noun
zhù cè zī jīn yě bú tài yán gé
注 册 资 金 也 不 太 严 格。
The **registration** capital is also not too strict.

1031 注射　　　　　zhù shè　　　**Verb:** to inject
　　　　　　　　　　　　　　　　　　Noun: injection

Verb
wǒ yào zhù shè liú gǎn yì miáo
我 要 **注 射** 流 感 疫 苗。
I am going **to get an injection** of the flu vaccine.

Noun
nǐ xiāng xìn zhù shè de xiào guǒ ma
你 相 信 **注 射** 的 效 果 吗？
Do you believe in the effectiveness of the **injection**?

1032 注视　zhù shì　**Verb:** to stare; to gaze

hěn duō kè rén dōu zài zhù shì tā de lǐ fú
很 多 客 人 都 在 **注 视** 她 的 礼 服。
Many guests were all **staring** at her attire.

1033 注重　zhù zhòng　**Verb:** to stress on; to pay attention to

dāng rán， tā tài tai yì zhí zhù zhòng chuān zhuó dǎ bàn
当 然， 他 太 太 一 直 **注 重** 穿 着 打 扮。
Of course, his wife always **pays attention to** attire and grooming.

1034 祝贺　zhù hè　**Verb:** to congratulate　**Noun:** congratulation

Verb

zhù hè nǐ men jié hūn èr shí zhōu nián
祝 贺 你 们 结 婚 二 十 周 年！
I **congratulate** you on your 20th wedding anniversary!

Noun

fēi cháng gǎn xiè nǐ men rè qíng de zhù hè
非 常 感 谢 你 们 热 情 的 **祝 贺**！
Thank you very much for your warm **congratulations**!

1035 专辑　zhuān jí　**Noun:** album

tīng shuō tā de zuì xīn zhuān jí mài le yì qiān wàn zhāng
听 说 他 的 最 新 **专 辑** 卖 了 一 千 万 张。
I heard that his latest **album** sold 10 million copies.

1036 专利　zhuān lì　**Noun:** patent

zhè jiā gōng sī shēn qǐng le yí xiàng xīn de zhuān lì
这 家 公 司 申 请 了 一 项 新 的 **专 利**。
This company has applied for a new **patent**.

1037 转化

zhuǎn huà

Verb: to transform
Noun: transformation

Verb

wǒ zài diàn shì shàng kàn jǐ qì rén zhuǎn huà
我 在 电 视 上 看 机 器 人 **转 化** 。
I'm watching robots **transforming** on TV.

Noun

tā men de zhuǎn huà sù dù chāo kuài
他 们 的 **转 化** 速 度 超 快 ！
Their **transformation** speed is super fast!

1038 转换

zhuǎn huàn

Verb: to convert
Noun: conversion

Verb

wǒ yào bǎ yīng bàng zhuǎn huàn chéng rén mín bì
我 要 把 英 镑 **转 换** 成 人 民 币 。
I want to **convert** British Pounds to Chinese Yuan.

Noun

qǐng wèn xiàn zài de zhuǎn huàn lǜ shì duō shǎo
请 问 现 在 的 **转 换** 率 是 多 少 ？
What is the current **conversion** rate?

1039 转让

zhuǎn ràng

Verb: to transfer
(objects, power or
ownership)
Noun: transfer

Verb

wǒ dǎ suàn bǎ gōng sī de gǔ fèn zhuǎn ràng gěi tā
我 打 算 把 公 司 的 股 份 **转 让** 给 她 。
I plan to **transfer** the company's shares to her.

Noun

tā tóng yì jiē shōu nǐ de zhuǎn ràng le ma
她 同 意 接 收 你 的 **转 让** 了 吗 ？
Has she agreed to receive your **transfer**?

1040 转向

zhuǎn xiàng

Verb: to move to;
to change direction

wǒ huì bǎ zī jīn zhuǎn xiàng zhǐ shù jī jīn
我 会 把 资 金 **转 向** 指 数 基 金 。
I will **move** my capital **into** index funds.

1041 装饰   zhuāng shì   **Verb:** to decorate
Noun: decoration

Verb
wǒ men zài yòng cǎi dēng zhuāng shì shèng dàn shù
我 们 在 用 彩 灯 **装 饰** 圣 诞 树 。
We are **decorating** the Christmas tree with colorful lights.

Noun
zhè xiē zhuāng shì què shí tài hǎo kàn le
这 些 **装 饰** 确 实 太 好 看 了 ！
These **decorations** are really beautiful!

1042 撞   zhuàng   **Verb:** to hit; to knock

zāo gāo xiǎo gǒu zhuàng dǎo shèng dàn lǐ wù le
糟 糕 ！ 小 狗 **撞** 倒 圣 诞 礼 物 了 。
Oops! The puppy **knocked** over the Christmas presents.

1043 资本   zī běn   **Noun:** capital (money)

wǒ de jīn róng kè chéng zhuān zhù zī běn guǎn lǐ
我 的 金 融 课 程 专 注 **资 本** 管 理 。
My finance course focuses on **capital** management.

1044 资产   zī chǎn   **Noun:** asset

zhè bāo kuò duì xiàn zī chǎn hé zhuǎn mài zī chǎn
这 包 括 兑 现 **资 产** 和 转 卖 **资 产** 。
This includes cashing out **assets** and reselling **assets**.

1045 资助   zī zhù   **Verb:** to sponsor; to give financial aid
Noun: sponsorship

Verb
tā yǐ gè rén míng yì zī zhù le cí shàn jī gòu
她 以 个 人 名 义 **资 助** 了 慈 善 机 构 。
She **sponsored** the charity in her personal capacity.

Noun
tā men hěn gǎn jī yǒu tā de zī zhù
他 们 很 感 激 有 她 的 **资 助** 。
They are grateful to have her **sponsorship**.

1046 子弹　zǐ dàn　　Noun: bullet

zhè shì dào jù qiāng, lǐ miàn méi yǒu zǐ dàn
这 是 道 具 枪, 里 面 没 有 **子 弹**。
This is a prop gun, there are no **bullets** in it.

1047 仔细　zǐ xì　　Adjective: careful
　　　　　　　　　　Adverb: carefully

Adj.
zài jià shǐ chē liàng fāng miàn, tā yì zhí hěn zǐ xì
在 驾 驶 车 辆 方 面, 他 一 直 很 **仔 细**。
In terms of driving vehicles, he's always been **careful**.

Adv.
nǐ kàn, wǒ zǐ xì jì lù le tā de jià shǐ guò chéng
你 看, 我 **仔 细** 记 录 了 他 的 驾 驶 过 程。
You see, I **carefully** recorded his driving process.

1048 紫　zǐ　　Adjective: purple

wǒ yǒu yí jiàn zǐ qí páo hé yí jiàn huáng hàn fú
我 有 一 件 **紫** 旗 袍 和 一 件 黄 汉 服。
I have a **purple** cheongsam and a yellow traditional Chinese dress.

1049 自豪　zì háo　　Adjective: proud

wǒ bàn yǎn huáng dì de shí hòu gǎn jué hěn zì háo
我 扮 演 皇 帝 的 时 候 感 觉 很 **自 豪**。
I feel very **proud** when I was playing the role of the emperor.

1050 自杀　zì shā　　Verb: to commit suicide

zhè gè lì shǐ rén wù shì zì shā de
这 个 历 史 人 物 是 **自 杀** 的。
This historical figure **committed suicide**.

1051 自愿 — zì yuàn — **Verb:** to be willing; to voluntarily do

tā dāng shí bú shì zì yuàn tuì wèi ér shì bèi bī de
他 当 时 不 是 **自 愿** 退 位 ，而 是 被 逼 的 。

At that time, he did not abdicate **voluntarily** but was forced to do so.

1052 总裁 — zǒng cái — **Noun:** CEO; president (company boss)

lián zǒng cái yě dú guò tā de zhuàn jì
连 **总 裁** 也 读 过 他 的 传 记 。

Even the **CEO** has read his biography.

1053 总数 — zǒng shù — **Noun:** sum; totality

zhè shì cái wù bù mén jì suàn de lì rùn zǒng shù
这 是 财 务 部 门 计 算 的 利 润 **总 数** 。

This is the **total** profit calculated by the finance department.

1054 总算 — zǒng suàn — **Adverb:** finally

tài hǎo le jīn nián de shōu rù zǒng suàn gāo le yí bèi
太 好 了 ！今 年 的 收 入 **总 算** 高 了 一 倍 。

Very good! This year's income has **finally** doubled.

1055 总体 — zǒng tǐ — **Noun:** overall; total

gè gè yè wù de biǎo xiàn zǒng tǐ mǎn yì
各 个 业 务 的 表 现 **总 体** 满 意 。

The performance of each business is satisfactory **overall**.

1056 阻碍   zǔ ài   **Verb:** to hamper; to block
Noun: obstacle

Verb

<small>tū rán de xì tǒng bēn kuì zǔ ài le xiàng mù yǎn shì</small>
突 然 的 系 统 奔 溃 **阻 碍** 了 项 目 演 示 。
A sudden system crash **hampered** the project demonstration.

Noun

<small>xī wàng wǒ men de xià yí gè yǎn shì méi yǒu zǔ ài</small>
希 望 我 们 的 下 一 个 演 示 没 有 **阻 碍** 。
I hope our next presentation encounters no **obstacles**.

1057 组织   zǔ zhī   **Verb:** to organize
Noun: organization

Verb

<small>wǒ yào zǔ zhī dà jiā qù cān guǎn qìng zhù</small>
我 要 **组 织** 大 家 去 餐 馆 庆 祝 。
I need to **organize** everyone to go to a restaurant to celebrate.

Noun

<small>zhè shì gōng sī de zǔ zhī jié gòu tú</small>
这 是 公 司 的 **组 织** 结 构 图 。
This is the company's **organization** structure chart.

1058 醉   zuì   **Verb:** to get drunk

<small>tā zài jù huì shàng zuì le yì zhí hú yán luàn yǔ</small>
他 在 聚 会 上 **醉** 了 ， 一 直 胡 言 乱 语 。
He **got drunk** at the party and kept talking nonsense.

1059 尊敬   zūn jìng   **Verb:** to respect (out of admiration)
Noun: respect

Verb

<small>wǒ men dōu hěn zūn jìng zhè wèi dǎo shī</small>
我 们 都 很 **尊 敬** 这 位 导 师 。
We all **respect** this mentor very much.

Noun

<small>tā yòng zhì huì hé kāng kǎi yíng dé le dà jiā de zūn jìng</small>
她 用 智 慧 和 慷 慨 赢 得 了 大 家 的 **尊 敬** 。
She won everyone's **respect** with her wisdom and generosity.

1060 尊重

zūn zhòng

Verb: to respect (out of acknowledgement)
Noun: respect

Verb

wǒ suī rán bù tóng yì， dàn zūn zhòng nǐ de guān diǎn
我 虽 然 不 同 意， 但 尊 重 你 的 观 点。
Although I disagree, I **respect** your point of view.

Noun

wǒ zhè yàng shuō shì wèi le biǎo shì duì nǐ de zūn zhòng
我 这 样 说 是 为 了 表 示 对 你 的 尊 重。
I say this as a way to show my **respect** for you.

1061 遵守

zūn shǒu

Verb: to abide by

rú guǒ nǐ bù xiǎng zūn shǒu guī dìng， kě yǐ suí shí lí kāi
如 果 你 不 想 遵 守 规 定，可 以 随 时 离 开。
If you don't want **to abide by** the rules, you can leave at any time.

2

KEY GRAMMAR
IN CONTEXT

① 到...为止

到 + time/event + 为 止
dào　　　　　　　　wéi zhǐ

to indicate a limit or endpoint in time or space
until/up to...

Ex. 1

总 裁 说 跟 他 们 的 合 作 到 此 为 止 。
zǒng cái shuō gēn tā men de hé zuò dào cǐ wéi zhǐ

The CEO said that the cooperation with them ends at (goes **up to**) this point.

Ex. 2

我 们 要 继 续 加 班 ，到 晚 上 八 点
wǒ men yào jì xù jiā bān　　　dào wǎn shàng bā diǎn
为 止 。
wéi zhǐ

We will continue to work overtime **until** 8pm.

Write your own:

② 对...而言

对 + subject + 而 言 + clause
duì　　　　　　　　ér yán

to express the perspective or opinion of a person or group
for...

Ex. 1

对 我 而 言 ，保 持 乐 观 很 重 要 。
duì wǒ ér yán　　bǎo chí lè guān hěn zhòng yào

For me, it's important to stay positive.

Ex. 2

对 中 方 而 言 ，实 现 双 赢 是 目 标 。
duì zhōng fāng ér yán　　shí xiàn shuāng yíng shì mù biāo

For (the side of) China, achieving a win-win situation is the goal.

Write your own:

204

③ 一方面...另一方面...

一 方面 +A+ 另 一 方面 +B
yì fāng miàn　　　 lìng yì fāng miàn

to present two contrasting or complementary aspects
on one hand... on the other hand...

Ex. 1

他 一 方面 想 创 业，另一方面 怕 挑 战。
tā yì fāng miàn xiǎng chuàng yè　 lìng yì fāng miàn pà tiǎo zhàn

On the one hand, he wants to start a business, but **on the other hand**, he's afraid of challenges.

Ex. 2

公 司 一 方面 要 节 约 成 本，另 一 方
gōng sī yì fāng miàn yào jié yuē chéng běn　 lìng yì fāng
面 要 扩 展 业 务。
miàn yào kuò zhǎn yè wù

On the one hand, the company wants to save costs, and **on the other hand**, it needs to expand its business.

Write your own:

④ 时而...时而...

时 而 +A+ 时 而 +B
shí ér　　　 shí ér

to describe actions or situations that alternate between two states
sometimes... sometimes...

Ex. 1

这 个 社 区 时而 安 静，时而 吵 闹。
zhè gè shè qū shí ér ān jìng　 shí ér chǎo nào

This community is **sometimes** quiet and **sometimes** noisy.

Ex. 2

她 情 绪 不 稳 定，时而 高 兴，时而
tā qíng xù bù wěn dìng　 shí ér gāo xìng shí ér
悲 伤。
bēi shāng

Her emotions are unstable, **sometimes** happy and **sometimes** sad.

Write your own:

205

⑤ 尽管...还是/但是...

尽^{jǐn}管^{guǎn} +condition+ 还^{hái}是^{shì}/但^{dàn}是^{shì} +result

to express a contrast between two statements
despite/even though... (but/still)...

Ex. 1

尽^{jǐn}管^{guǎn}分^{fēn}手^{shǒu}了^{le}，我^{wǒ}们^{men}还^{hái}是^{shì}好^{hǎo}朋^{péng}友^{yǒu}。

Even though we broke up, we are **still** good friends.

Ex. 2

尽^{jǐn}管^{guǎn}被^{bèi}处^{chǔ}罚^{fá}，但^{dàn}是^{shì}他^{tā}没^{méi}有^{yǒu}向^{xiàng}任^{rèn}何^{hé}人^{rén}抱^{bào}怨^{yuàn}。

Despite being punished, (**but**) he didn't complain to anyone.

Write your own:

⑥ 既然...就...

既^{jì}然^{rán} +condition+ 就^{jiù} +result

to express a logical conclusion that naturally follows from a given situation
since... then...

Ex. 1

既^{jì}然^{rán}结^{jié}婚^{hūn}了^{le}，你^{nǐ}以^{yǐ}后^{hòu}就^{jiù}别^{bié}和^{hé}前^{qián}女^{nǚ}友^{yǒu}联^{lián}系^{xì}。

Since you're married, **then** don't contact your ex-girlfriend from now on.

Ex. 2

既^{jì}然^{rán}你^{nǐ}们^{men}已^{yǐ}经^{jīng}达^{dá}成^{chéng}协^{xié}议^{yì}，我^{wǒ}就^{jiù}不^{bù}担^{dān}心^{xīn}了^{le}。

Since you've reached an agreement, (**then**) I don't worry any more.

Write your own:

⑦ 只有...才...

只 有 + condition + 才 + result

_{cái}

emphasizes the necessity of a particular condition for a certain result to occur
only... can...

Ex. 1
zhǐ yǒu zhāng wén cái néng shú liàn de shǐ yòng zhè gè ruǎn jiàn
只 有 张 文 才 能 熟 练 地 使 用 这 个 软 件。
Only Zhang Wen **can** use this software skilfully.

Ex. 2
yé ye shuō zhǐ yǒu tōng guò zhè gè kǎo yàn cái néng jì
爷 爷 说 只 有 通 过 这 个 考 验 才 能 继
chéng tā de cái chǎn
承 他 的 财 产。
Grandpa said that **only** by passing this test **can** one inherit his property.

Write your own:

⑧ 不论...只/都...

bú lùn
不 论 + condition + 只 / 都 + result

_{zhǐ dōu}

to express the idea of universality or invariance under different conditions
regardless of... always/only...

Ex. 1
bú lùn nǐ xiāng bù xiāng xìn wǒ zhǐ ài nǐ yí gè rén
不 论 你 相 不 相 信，我 只 爱 你 一 个 人。
Regardless of whether you believe it or not, I **only** love you alone.

Ex. 2
bú lùn tā zěn me dǎ ban tā dōu bù néng xī yǐn
不 论 她 怎 么 打 扮 ， 她 都 不 能 吸 引
tā de zhù yì
他 的 注 意。
Regardless of how she dressed up, she (**always**) couldn't attract his attention.

Write your own:

⑨ 不管...反正...

bù guǎn
不 管 + conditions + **反 正** + result
fǎn zhèng

to express a disregard for certain conditions or circumstances
regardless/no matter... anyway...

Ex. 1

bù guǎn guì bu guì fǎn zhèng nǐ bì xū zì jǐ zū fáng zhù
不 管 贵 不 贵，反 正 你 必 须 自 己 租 房 住。
Regardless of whether it's expensive or not, you must rent a place to live on your own **anyway**.

Ex. 2

bù guǎn jiǎng lì shì shén me nǐ yí dìng yào jìn lì
不 管 奖 励 是 什 么， 你 一 定 要 尽 力
wán chéng bǐ sài
完 成 比 赛。
No matter what the reward is, you must do your best to complete the competition **anyway**.

Write your own:

⑩ 受...爱戴

shòu   **ài dài**
A + **受** + B + **爱 戴**

to be loved or adored by a particular group or community
loved by...

Ex. 1

zhè gè guó jiā de qián zǒng tǒng hěn shòu rén mín de ài dài
这 个 国 家 的 前 总 统 很 **受** 人 民 的 **爱 戴**。
The ex-president of this country was very **loved by** its people.

Ex. 2

tā juān le yì bǎi wàn měi yuán hòu shòu dào le cí shàn
他 捐 了 一 百 万 美 元 后 **受** 到 了 慈 善
jī gòu de ài dài
机 构 的 **爱 戴**。
After he donated 1 million dollars, he was **loved by** the charity.

Write your own:

⑪ 跟...相比

A + 跟 (gēn) + B + 相比 (xiāng bǐ) + clause

to make a comparison between two entities, situations, or concepts
compared to...

Ex. 1
我 的 狗 **跟** 其 他 狗 **相 比** ， 非 常 胆 小 。
wǒ de gǒu gēn qí tā gǒu xiāng bǐ fēi cháng dǎn xiǎo

Compared to other dogs, my dog is very timid.

Ex. 2
跟 和 朋 友 聚 餐 **相 比** ， 参 加 你 的 毕
gēn hé péng yǒu jù cān xiāng bǐ cān jiā nǐ de bì
业 典 礼 更 重 要 。
yè diǎn lǐ gèng zhòng yào

Compared to having dinner with friends, attending your graduation ceremony is more important.

Write your own:

⑫ 受...影响

A + 受 (shòu) + B + 影响 (yǐng xiǎng)

to indicate the influence of one thing on another
under the influence of...

Ex. 1
受 她 的 **影 响** ， 我 爱 上 了 弹 钢 琴 。
shòu tā de yǐng xiǎng wǒ ài shàng le tán gāng qín

Under her **influence**, I fell in love with playing the piano.

Ex. 2
受 这 本 书 的 **影 响** ， 我 开 始 和 好 友
shòu zhè běn shū de yǐng xiǎng wǒ kāi shǐ hé hǎo yǒu
分 享 感 想 。
fēn xiǎng gǎn xiǎng

Influenced by this book, I began to share my thoughts with good friends.

Write your own:

⑬ 自从...就...

zì cóng
自 从 + time/event + 就 jiù + action

to indicate something has been the case since a particular time or event
ever since... (then)

Ex. 1

zì cóng qù nián bā yuè wǒ jiù shēn shēn de ài shàng le tā
自 从 去 年 八 月，我 就 深 深 地 爱 上 了 他。

Ever since last August, I have been deeply in love with him.

Ex. 2

zì cóng dìng hūn hòu wǒ men jiù dǎ suàn yì qǐ mǎi
自 从 订 婚 后，我 们 就 打 算 一 起 买
fáng zi
房 子。

Ever since we got engaged, we've been planning to buy a house together.

Write your own:

⑭ 从...的角度(来)看

cóng
从 + someone + de jiǎo dù lái kàn 的 角 度 来 看 + clause

from the perspective of...

Ex. 1

cóng tā de jiǎo dù lái kàn xiàng yín háng dài kuǎn shì
从 她 的 角 度 来 看，向 银 行 贷 款 是
wéi yī de xuǎn zé
唯 一 的 选 择。

From her **perspective**, taking out a loan from the bank is the only option.

Ex. 2

cóng nián qīng rén de jiǎo dù kàn jié hūn bú shì rén
从 年 轻 人 的 角 度 看，结 婚 不 是 人
shēng bì xū de
生 必 需 的。

From the perspective of young people, marriage is not a necessity in life.

Write your own:

210

yóu yú
由 于 + cause + effect

to express causation or reason behind an event, situation, or outcome
due to...

Ex. 1

yóu yú yào wù guò mǐn   tā yǒu le tóu yūn de zhèng zhuàng
由 于 药 物 过 敏， 她 有 了 头 晕 的 症 状。
Due to an allergic reaction to medication, she experienced symptoms of dizziness.

Ex. 2

yóu yú gōng sī bèi jiān bìng le   hěn duō tóng shì bèi cái le
由 于 公 司 被 兼 并 了， 很 多 同 事 被 裁 了。
Due to the company being merged, many colleagues were laid off.

Write your own:

---

shǒu xiān   qí cì   zuì hòu
首 先 + A + 其 次 + B + 最 后 + C

to organize and present multiple points or steps in a logical order
first... then... last (finally)...

Ex. 1

shǒu xiān wǒ men yào qù zhōng guó   qí cì qù rì běn
首 先 我 们 要 去 中 国， 其 次 去 日 本，
zuì hòu qù hán guó
最 后 去 韩 国。
First we are going to China, **then** to Japan, and **finally** to South Korea.

Ex. 2

shǒu xiān tā shì gè fù qin   qí cì tā shì gè zhàng
首 先 他 是 个 父 亲， 其 次 他 是 个 丈
fu   zuì hòu tā shì guó jiā de shǒu xiàng
夫， 最 后 他 是 国 家 的 首 相。
First he is a father, **then** he is a husband, **last** he is the Prime Minister of his country.

Write your own:

⑰ ...被称为/作...

bèi chēng wéi zuò
A + 被 称 为 / 作 + B

to introduce a title or designation
...known as/regarded as...

Ex. 1

zhàn zhēng shèng lì hòu wáng jiāng jūn bèi dà jiā chēng wéi zhàn shén
战 争 胜 利 后，王 将 军 **被** 大 家 **称** **为** 战 神。

After the victory of the war, General Wang was **regarded as** the God of War by everyone.

Ex. 2

yīn wèi tiān tiān dǔ bó tā bèi lín jū men chēng zuò méi
因 为 天 天 赌 博，他 **被** 邻 居 们 **称** **作** 没
jiù de dǔ guǐ
救 的 赌 鬼。

Because he gambles every day, he is **known as** the Hopeless Gambler by his neighbors.

Write your own:

⑱ 向...推荐...

xiàng tuī jiàn
A + 向 + B + 推 荐 + object

to suggest or recommend something to someone
recommend... to...

Ex. 1

jǐ nián qián wǒ gē xiàng wǒ tuī jiàn le zhè fèn fān yì gōng zuò
几 年 前 我 哥 **向** 我 **推 荐** 了 这 份 翻 译 工 作。

A few years ago, my brother **recommended** this translation job **to** me.

Ex. 2

tā xiàng wǒ tuī jiàn jiā rù xué shēng huì de shèng dàn jié
她 **向** 我 **推 荐** 加 入 学 生 会 的 圣 诞 节
qìng zhù huó dòng
庆 祝 活 动。

She **recommended** me **to** join the Student Union Christmas celebrations.

Write your own:

⑲ 在...程度上...

zài
在 + modifier + 程度上 chéng dù shàng + clause

to indicate the degree or extent to
which something happens or is true
in terms of... / to some extent...

Ex. 1

zài zhuān yè chéng dù shàng　　　tā de gōng zuò néng lì fēi
在专业程度上，他的工作能力非
cháng chū sè
常出色。

In terms of professionalism, his work abilities are outstanding.

Ex. 2

tā men de xīn lǐ jiàn kāng zài yí dìng chéng dù shàng bèi
他们的心理健康在一定程度上被
fù mǔ hū lüè le
父母忽略了。

Their mental health has been neglected by their parents **to some extent**.

Write your own:

⑳ 不过是...罢了

bú guò shì
不过是 + description + 罢了 bà le

to downplay or minimize the
significance of something
just... nothing more

Ex. 1

zhè bú guò shì gè xiǎo shī wù bà le　　nǐ bú yòng dān xīn
这不过是个小失误罢了,你不用担心。

This is **just** a small error, **nothing more**, no need to worry.

Ex. 2

tā men bú guò shì chǎo jià shuō qì huà bà le　　bú
他们不过是吵架说气话罢了，不
huì zhēn de lí hūn
会真的离婚。

They are **just** arguing and speaking in anger, **nothing more**, they
are not really going to get divorced.

Write your own:

ACCESS AUDIO

Please follow the instructions provided below to access the Chinese audio for this book:

INSTRUCTIONS TO ACCESS AUDIO

1. **Scan this QR code**
    or go to: **www.linglingmandarin.com/books**

2. Locate this book in the list of LingLing Mandarin Books

3. Click the "Access Audio" button

4. Enter the password:

HYA33

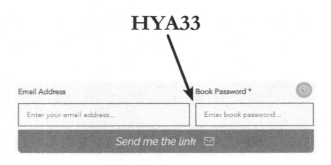

NEW HSK VOCABULARY SERIES

LEARN CHINESE
VOCABULARY FOR
BEGINNERS:
NEW HSK 1

LEARN CHINESE
VOCABULARY FOR
BEGINNERS:
NEW HSK 2

LEARN CHINESE
VOCABULARY FOR
BEGINNERS:
NEW HSK 3

LEARN CHINESE
VOCABULARY FOR
INTERMEDIATE:
NEW HSK 4

LEARN CHINESE
VOCABULARY FOR
INTERMEDIATE:
NEW HSK 5

LEARN CHINESE
VOCABULARY FOR
INTERMEDIATE:
NEW HSK 6

Get notified about **new releases**
https://linglingmandarin.com/notify

BOOKS BY LINGLING

**CHINESE
CONVERSATIONS**
FOR BEGINNERS

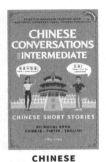

**CHINESE
CONVERSATIONS**
FOR INTERMEDIATE

MANDARIN WRITING
PRACTICE BOOK

CHINESE STORIES
FOR LANGUAGE
LEARNERS:
ELEMENTARY

CHINESE STORIES
FOR LANGUAGE
LEARNERS:
INTERMEDIATE

THE ART OF WAR
FOR LANGUAGE
LEARNERS

Get notified about **new releases**
https://linglingmandarin.com/notify

ABOUT THE AUTHOR

LingLing is a native Chinese Mandarin educator with an MA in Communication and Language. Originally from China, now living in the UK, she is the founder of the learning brand LingLing Mandarin, which aims to create the best resources for learners to master the Chinese language and achieve deep insight into Chinese culture in a fun and illuminating way. *Discover more about LingLing and access more great resources by following the links below or scanning the QR codes.*

 WEBSITE
linglingmandarin.com

YOUTUBE
youtube.com/c/linglingmandarin

 PATREON
patreon.com/linglingmandarin

INSTAGRAM
instagram.com/linglingmandarin

Made in the USA
Las Vegas, NV
10 June 2024

90968231R00125